THE
EMPTY
NEST
BLUEPRINT
for
SINGLE PARENTS

Praise for Anthony Damaschino

"When your daughter is 3 it seems impossible that she will one day be 18 and off to college. Alas, the day has come, and time did pass too quickly as I was warned, and now I'm clinging to our final moments together. Thanks to *The Empty Nest Blueprint for Single Parents*, we've had crucial conversations about money and communication. As I prepare for this transition, I'm grateful for the guidance and tools provided in this thoughtful and well-organized book. Though our household will soon be missing one member, I know our bond will endure. Thank you, Anthony Damaschino, for helping navigate this new chapter in both our lives."

—Shelby Bybee, Co-host of the *Dear Midlife* Podcast

"Don't read another article or listen to any other podcast on this topic! Anthony Damaschino has done all the listening, reading, analyzing, comparing, contrasting and heavy lifting we single parents typically do all on our own. With this book, companionship weaves its way into, as Anthony calls it, this underrated stage of life. As a single parent, empty nester, and family therapist, this book serves as my handbook, my support system, my cheerleader, my partner during a chapter when flying solo can be its hardest. After reading and referring to this book time and again, I feel applauded, seen and supported as a parent who typically muscles the strength of two. With each turn of the page, my shoulders softened, my grip lessened, and my nest no longer felt empty, but reshaped, confident, still cozy, and still available. My nest, a beautifully built haven for my own solo flight."

—Beth Clardy Lewis, LPC-S; Author of *Stop Talking About Your Childhood: One Therapist's Personal Memoir & 21-day Strategy for Strengthening Adulthood, and Focusing Forward, Forever*

"Raising kids as a single mom is a whirlwind of love, late nights, and fierce determination. *The Empty Nest Blueprint for Single Parents* feels like seeing your own story reflected back at you while helping you prepare for your next stage in life. It provides practical tools and a roadmap for navigating the emotional rollercoaster of the empty nest. You'll discover you're not alone, and you can create a fulfilling future for yourself – one chapter at a time."

—Natalie Anderson, Founder, Mama's Got Grit

THE
EMPTY
NEST
BLUEPRINT
for
SINGLE PARENTS

Navigate Your New Normal and Thrive
for the Most Underrated Stage of Your Life

ANTHONY DAMASCHINO

The Empty Nest Blueprint for Single Parents
First edition June 2024

Infinite Space Publishing
Danville, California 94526
www.anthonydamaschino.com

ISBN Hardcover: 979-8-9885446-4-7
ISBN Paperback: 979-8-9885446-3-0
ISBN Ebook: 979-8-9885446-5-4
First Printing

Printed in the United States of America
10 9 8 7 6 5 4 3 2 1

Single parents defy expectations daily by juggling work, childcare, and emotional support for their families. Their strength and resilience are a testament to human potential, pushing the boundaries of what we can achieve. To all the single empty nesters, may your Empty Nest Blueprint bring you the excitement, fun, and joy you deserve!

TABLE OF CONTENTS

PREFACE. xi

INTRODUCTION 1

Chapter 1   The Empty Nest Realization 5

Chapter 2   The Average Single Empty Nester. 29

Chapter 3   You, The Empty Nester. 53

Chapter 4   Empty Nest Syndrome 73

Chapter 5   Symptoms to Solutions 99

Chapter 6   Parenting DNA 127

Chapter 7   Parent-Child to Parent-Adult 149

Chapter 8   Pre-Launch Advice .173

Chapter 9   The Uniqueness of Being a Single
             Empty Nester 193

Chapter 10   Empty Nest Threats 211

Chapter 11   Empty Nest Threat #4—Deprioritization . .233

Chapter 12   Empty Nest Opportunities. 257

Chapter 13   Create Your Blueprint, Part 1. 273

Chapter 14   It's Achievable 297

Chapter 15   Your Plan for You, Part 2 313

Chapter 16   Your Plan for Your Child, Part 3 337

CONCLUSION. 361

AFTERWORD 365

ACKNOWLEDGMENTS. 367

NOTES 369

ABOUT THE AUTHOR 375

PREFACE

MY PURPOSE FOR writing my first book, *The Empty Nest Blueprint*, was to help individuals transition through this life stage. My goal has always been to help a parent or parents become aware of their Empty Nest journey, avoid pitfalls, and experience this transition as positively as possible. Most of my research and the data I collected, including threats and opportunities, applied to all Empty Nest parents undergoing this process.

However, as I dove further into the Empty Nest topic, it became increasingly apparent that one's Empty Nest journey as a single parent versus a parent with a partner to experience the journey with had some significant differences. The empty nester who was married or in a full-time relationship would be going through the emotional and physical process of their child leaving with someone by their side. In this scenario, there are personal relationship negatives to overcome, such as marital strife, partner drift, parenting conflicts, and post-child departure adjustment as a couple. Conversely, the positive Empty Nest opportunities include reconnecting with a spouse, focusing on the couple relationship, and planning a future together.

On the contrary, the single empty nester would be going through the emotional and physical process of their child leaving alone. In this scenario, there are potentially more significant challenges, such as the emotional impact of a child leaving, the single parent–child relationship, self-discovery, and management as a single empty nester. Topics such as these are different than those of an empty nesting couple.

When writing a book, an author inevitably needs to make choices. For example, do I want to discuss boomerang children (kids that come back to the nest), children who never leave the nest, and multigenerational households, to name just a few? In *The Empty Nest Blueprint*, I made strategic decisions to focus on all empty nesters, as individuals and parents, as well as on a spouse and the relationship as a couple. As soon as I made that decision, I knew I would have to write *The Empty Nest Blueprint for Single Parents*. In my first book, I set aside single-parent-focused research and cut any single-parent narrative, knowing this day would come. I felt so strongly about this that *The Empty Nest Blueprint* had yet to be published when I started writing this book.

In this book, I took all of the applicable Empty Nest data, examples, and lessons from the first book and purged all spouse and couple-centric chapters. Doing this enabled me to include the research, observations, and recommendations uniquely applicable to a single parent in the Empty Nest stage of their life. This book wasn't written for all empty nesters. This book was written for you, a single parent going through or entering your Empty Nest transition.

INTRODUCTION

IF YOU PUT yourself on the back burner, you will still get burned. It just takes longer.

Whether making a bed, cleaning out your car, or creating a blueprint for the rest of your life, you are better off spending a little more time with an incremental effort to succeed. There is a saying, "Anything worth doing is worth doing well." This is no exception for your Empty Nest journey. I'm not sure when it happened, but sometime in my adult experience, when I wasn't at work, I plowed through the weekend to-do items like a mad person. I raced around running errands, chauffeuring my children everywhere, and knocking out the endless list of things that needed to get done. I'm not saying I half-assed everything, but volume and completion seemed more critical than connection and quality.

As parents, we often make these choices. Children first. With chores, it's no big deal; we can get it done. With our self-care, it can be unforgivable. In a detailed survey of numerous single Empty Nest parents, which I will refer to throughout this book, one big takeaway was that time spent on parenting, work, and the day-to-day life routine often left the single parent without any dedicated time for themselves. On the occasions where there was time, it was sporadic and quickly interrupted by other responsibilities. Prioritizing oneself was placed on the single parent's back burner. It doesn't have to be this way. Becoming an empty nester is an opportunity to embrace change, pivot from a life of putting others and responsibilities first, and focus on doing your own life well. As a parent of three and a current empty nester, I struggled when my journey started. But as I explored everything about an Empty Nest, I pulled from all the information I could find and found a path toward creating my best future. This book will help you do just that.

Over the following chapters, you will learn what every parent should know about their Empty Nest transition. You will learn about Empty Nest Syndrome, as well as both the symptoms and the solutions. You will explore the threats you face and the opportunities you embrace. You will gain insights into your past, evaluate your relationship with your child, and work through the present to prepare for this next stage in life. Beyond knowledge and understanding, we will do something great together. We will create your Empty Nest Blueprint, essentially a roadmap of your future, filled with excitement, fun, and joy. Your blueprint will not only map out the future you want, but it will contain minimally two distinct plans to ensure you are ideally prepared to grow and evolve as a parent and a person.

I am excited to share my journey, research, and the single-parent Empty Nest perspective on this topic. I look forward to helping you build your best Empty Nest future. The time is now to figure out what you want your future to be and how you can make that a reality.

> *"Being a single parent is not a life full of struggles, but a journey for the strong."*
>
> —MEG LOWREY

CHAPTER ONE

The Empty Nest Realization

SOME THINGS IN life are out in the open, such as your name, what you do for a living, and whether you have children. You offer these three facts freely to people you have just met, the checker at the grocery store, or anyone who asks. On the other hand, there are the private parts of our lives. These things you keep to yourself won't be asked by someone you just met, and no matter how much you love having your groceries rung up by Dean, your favorite checker, he'll never know.

Being an empty nester isn't taboo. It's not a secret. It's not even highly debated. However, the emotional journey and process of becoming an empty nester is one many of us experience silently in our thoughts. Dean may ask about your children while ringing up the mayonnaise you like. You may offer up that your child will be going off to college in the fall. But after Dean asks where they are going, congratulates you on becoming an empty nester, and hands you your receipt, your Empty Nest discussion is over.

The prior example shows how Empty Nest conversations go for most people. For many of us, this is what being an empty nester is today—a short conversation, a party punchline, a dismissed rite of passage, or a label someone assigns to us. You have reached a milestone no different from the experience of generations of parents before you. You created a family, your child or children are edging toward adulthood, and you are on the precipice of your last child leaving the nest. Although this is a fantastic eighteen-plus-year accomplishment on your part, you won't get a cake with candles on it. There is no hallmark card on the shelf wishing congratulations, and you surely don't get the day off work. Becoming an empty nester is a rite of passage where all eyes seem to be focused on the child leaving the nest and not the parent left behind.

What seems like a minor change or a dismissive label is one of a parent's most unrecognized and complex periods. The culmination of child-rearing, parenting, and a significant focus on your life's purpose is about to change. Whether you know it or not, you are in a transformational stage. Unknown threats lie ahead, as well as potential opportunities to seize. At the very least, your relationship with your child will change. The idea of your sense of self and the dynamic in your household is about to pivot. Your identity as an active parent, a chauffeur, a cook, and an ATM will be forever changed. Well, maybe not the ATM part, but all other child and family-focused activities will likely evolve.

As your children leave the nest and go on to live their best lives, you too can build your best Empty Nest life. But what no one has bothered to tell you is that everything good about becoming an empty nester doesn't just naturally happen. In fact, without a blueprint in place, you may find yourself missing out on developing the life you want and the relationships you desire.

In this book, *The Empty Nest Blueprint for Single Parents,* you will learn to plan, pursue, and thrive for what I consider one of life's most underrated stages. As you read and experience each chapter, you will prepare for this critical transition. By the end of our time together, you will not only gain knowledge and tools to understand your Empty Nest journey ahead, but you also will be in a position to ensure the best outcome for your well-being, your child, and your Empty Nest future.

Becoming an empty nester isn't reduced to a check-out counter conversation with Dean but rather the start of you living your best Empty Nest life.

The Empty Nest Label

There is no definitive answer as to when the term "Empty Nest" started. The definition undoubtedly comes from birds whose offspring leave the nest when they reach maturity. Unlike humans, this transition is relatively easy for birds since, according to The World Animal Foundation, "Most baby birds will leave their nests within a few weeks. However, some bird species will stay in their nests for up to six weeks before fledging (leaving the nest)." Since the act of offspring leaving the nest is natural, we undoubtedly stole the term. We adopted it to represent a home or a family where the children have gone, but the similarities between birds and people end there. For humans, nest bonding isn't a few-week exercise that ends quickly but rather an ambitious two decades of caring, feeding, and guiding our human babies into young adulthood.

It's fantastic that, after eighteen years of care in the human language and culture, the term "Empty Nest" doesn't hold more weight. Like many terms tossed about (i.e., middle age or stay-at-home labels), there is no seriousness or general acknowledgment when one becomes an empty nester. For most people, becoming an empty nester is not given much thought or credence.

Beneath the casual label, there is something more severe and permanent. Your status as an active parent is changing. Your children are leaving the nest, so a new label is afforded to you. Make no mistake, like many labels you have been branded with in the past (adult, single, parent), this label is just as impactful as the others. Becoming an empty nester defines the next stage in your life. All changes in life status come with actions, emotions, and self-contemplation as we move into something different—for example, the transition of becoming a parent. You likely experienced nine months of pregnancy directly or indirectly, which involved preparation, organization, and acceptance. This one life-changing example involved you dedicating time, energy, and thought to the preparation for your experience to become something new (a parent). Life changes are milestone events worthy of your focus and time. Becoming an empty nester is no different.

Your Labels

Labels are a fascinating thing. They intend to communicate an attribute or characteristic of a person quickly and concisely. Whether you have thought about it or not, you have been labeled many things throughout your lifetime. You have been a baby, a child, and an adolescent. You became a teenager, a young adult, and then an adult. Each label came with expectations, challenges, and a new sense of self. As a baby, perhaps things were a bit easier. You cried, you slept, and you were fed. You were expected to learn, pay attention, listen, and follow the rules as a child. As a teen, you were expected to take on responsibility, follow a moral code, and mature. As an adult, you were expected to become self-reliant, make good decisions, and be responsible. These one-word labels carry attributes, characteristics, and expectations with them.

Labels are not just calendar-driven, defining how old you are; they are often associated with your next step in personal development. For example, labels like teammate, student, and coworker aren't age-based. As you grow up, you are assigned or achieve labels defining where you are in life.

There are a series of other labels associated with you. These labels didn't just happen to you over the ordinary course of time; instead, you made life choices as an adult to become them. A good example is when you went from being single to being in a relationship and perhaps back to being single again. This is your relationship status, but it's just another label. Keeping on the same trajectory, with the arrival of your first child, your label changed to a family. And if we want to attach a few more descriptive labels to having a child, you became a parent, a mother or father, a primary caregiver, a working parent, a stay-at-home dad, an active parent, etc.

Your list of labels is pretty impressive and continues to evolve as you accomplish lifetime milestones. You have labels referencing your generation, such as Gen Z or Millennial, and labels describing choices you made at each stage of life, such as a career title or study area. Finally, wrapping up the never-ending label example, you undoubtedly have a few more big label changes in your future. For example, you will probably evolve from working to retired, from parent to grand-parent, from a household with children to an empty nester.

Why is the realization of your labels or a change in your life stage so significant? It's crucial because these critical transitions in life, although exciting and monumental, can also be time-consuming, complex, and stress-inducing. For example:

- A high school or college graduation fits all the descriptors. It takes years of hard work and planning, and there is an endless list of things to learn and do. There are educational pressures, social pressures, and never-ending assignments to ensure they get done.
- Pregnancy is a big life transition. The nesting process can include nursery preparation, required reading, anxiety over the health of the mother and baby, and adaptation to physical changes.
- Retirement fits the life stage descriptor. Retirement is seen as monumental and exciting, but it is filled with work to get there and stress around managing money, time, and a lifestyle as one ages.

These three milestone labels are each considered positive, so friends, family, and society often celebrate them. However, we also know that each of these milestones can stress relationships, be fraught with emotions, and bring uncertainty and anxiety. The same explanation can be applied to becoming an empty nester.

The most common advice for anyone facing a significant life stage change is to prepare, plan, read, anticipate, and connect with others to help with the upcoming change. Let's quickly do our first reflection exercise.

Exercise 1 – Time & Effort

Directions: Below are three questions, each followed by a further explanation. Read each, consider the time spent, and focus on each topic.

Start: Ready? Go.

- **Graduation:** How much time did you spend working toward and mentally attaining your academic achievements?

  - Think of all the time you spent in a classroom, the homework, the social interaction. Think about the liked and disliked subjects, experiences, and emotions that came with each school year.

- **Pregnancy:** How much time did you spend thinking about becoming a parent and preparing to have a child?

  - Did you spend time thinking and preparing to get pregnant? Even if you didn't think about pre-pregnancy, as a future mother or father, you likely had nine months to focus on your upcoming life change.

- **Retirement:** How much time and effort have you put into or thought about your retirement?

▫ This is a topic for another book, but you have
  had years to plan and save for your retirement.
  Retirement is one of the top three worries of
  single-parent empty nesters (personal health and
  a child's health and well-being are the other two).

Ultimately, most big life transitions come with time to plan,
reflect, and prepare. What makes becoming an empty nester
different from the prior examples is that it is socially passive,
not seriously discussed, and usually kept somewhat private.
Most people don't prepare for their Empty Nest stage and
beyond. Most don't consider or recognize it as a milestone life
event. This is a big mistake.

In the end, becoming an empty nester is just a label,
and like all labels, it can be as innocent as a word. Still, labels
can also be daunting, carrying the weight of expectations,
experiences, and status. Your Empty Nest label and status are
as important and impactful as the other life milestone labels
you have been afforded.

More Than You

Becoming an empty nester starts with you. It involves
accepting a new routine where your time is no longer focused
on active parenting but on yourself. It requires you to explore
and understand your emotions and feelings as you focus less
on your child and more on yourself. In the best-case scenario,

your Empty Nest journey will have positive outcomes due to your actions. You are at the center of your journey and have the power to avoid the missteps and pitfalls of the unprepared empty nesters. This journey starts with you.

If you have an ex, becoming an empty nester also involves and impacts your former spouse. Regardless of your relationship with your ex, two legal deadlines are usually triggered during this period: child custody and child support. Most states in the United States end child custody when a child turns eighteen. In a few states, this eighteen-year rule ceases when a child gets married, joins the military, or dies. As for child support, the eighteen-year rule also applies; child support can cease if a child gets married or joins the military. However, multiple "special circumstances" exist in different states for child support to continue. For example, support may continue if a child is still in high school beyond eighteen or, as in New York, child support is extended until a child reaches the age of twenty-one. Additionally, child support may continue in some states if the child attends and incurs college expenses or if they have special needs.

Beyond the financial and legal considerations, discontinuing these obligations can also trigger closure or the finality of a relationship, making ongoing communication with an ex less frequent or stop altogether. Perhaps this is a welcome change during this Empty Nest phase.

If the relationship between parents is still close, they can be considered close friends going through an Empty Nest transition. They will each have their own unique journey. As individuals, we are different in our thoughts, emotions, and how we handle life and stress. It is impossible to assume or anticipate what your ex or a friend may be going through during their Empty Nest journey. In most cases, a default assumption is that they are okay and that their transition to becoming an empty nester is no big deal. As we dive deeper into this topic in the following chapters, you will find this is often untrue. Your ex or friend's experience, thoughts, and viewpoint may be similar, but it is dangerous to assume anything. You may be emotionally okay with everything going on while your ex struggles in silence. You may be aware of the changes around you and miss your child but not realize the weight of their experience. The bad news is you cannot read minds. The good news is you can become better equipped to communicate, understand, and react to the changes you and others will be going through.

A great start on your journey would be having your friends or ex read this book and prepare for their transition. However, as I will repeat throughout this book, your Empty Nest journey is about what you will learn and do, not what anyone else needs to do. You cannot make your ex, friend, or family prepare for their journey, just as you can't force them to read this book. However, you can be assured that after reading this book, you will be knowledgeable about the Empty Nest transition and will be able to share your experience and understanding of this topic. Additionally, you will be able to better understand and empathize with others going through this stage in life.

There is at least one other participant in the Empty Nest journey: your child or children. Becoming an empty nester may not directly involve your child, but they are part of the equation. When your child leaves the nest, you will no longer be actively parenting or managing their school, activities, calendar, and relationships. As previously stated, these changes affect you and your routine. However, the frequency and familiar day-to-day cohabiting relationship you have grown accustomed to will also change for your child. The physical change will probably lead to a change in the relationship between you and your child. As your child takes on more personal growth and responsibility outside the home, they will become less reliant and dependent on you. As your child's confidence and independence build, they may need you less, be more apt to figure things out for themselves, and start living a life that you are less attuned to and involved in.

In most cases, your new Empty Nest lifestyle is something your child may be oblivious to. Any personal struggles or changes you will face may be out of your child's sight. As your child is busy adjusting to their new independent lifestyle without you, you will do the same back home in parallel. Emotions, feelings, and life adjustments will happen to you both, but they will be experienced separately and from very different perspectives. Dr. Jessica Sosso, Family Medicine, Mayo Clinic Health System, said, "It's common for parents to find letting go to be a painful experience - even though they actively encourage their children to be independent."

Although your child and your Empty Nest situation can be filled with new beginnings and excitement, parents are more susceptible to sadness and loss as the parents are left behind. We will dive much deeper into this topic in chapter 2.

Parents are more susceptible to feelings of sadness and loss, as it is the parents that are left behind.

Beyond you and your child, all the empty nesters before you and those who come after you will each experience a unique yet not altogether different journey. Your friends and family members, peers and coworkers, and all individuals who experience their children leaving the home will undoubtedly share some attributes with you throughout their journey. There will be moments of stress, excitement, sadness, and fun. Most assuredly, they will experience change.

Change

From the casual observer's point of view, becoming an empty nester is built up to be a happy, proud, and rewarding moment of a parent's life. You had a child, you raised a child, and the eighteen-year developmental exercise now pays off as you launch your child into the world as an adult. From the casual observer's perspective, everything looks good.

The casual observer doesn't see the other changes happening around you. They don't see your child testing boundaries and adjusting to the new responsibilities and expectations. They don't see the emotional loss of daily parenting, the questioning of your new role as a parent, or the redefining of your sense of self. They don't see the self-doubt and uncertainty of the future.

Heraclitus, an ancient Greek philosopher, says, "There is nothing permanent except change." Daily, we experience changes in relationships, ourselves, and the world around us. Looking back at life changes, there is no more excellent example of personal change than when we became a parent. Becoming a parent is a generational turning point that changes every aspect of your life. When you became a parent, you signed up for the lifelong responsibility of the love, actions, and pressure of parenting. You evolved by applying everything you knew and had to raise a child. When your child leaves the nest, a significant shift and personal change happens again. You become an empty nester.

> **"Looking back at life changes, there is no greater example of personal change than when we became a parent."**

Contrary to what you may think about becoming an empty nester, this stage in life is real, vulnerable, and complex. Your sense of purpose, your routine, and the relationship you have with your child will change. This change is not unique to you; this change is also happening to your child in parallel. This can be a time of change with endless possibilities as you deepen relationships and plan for a fantastic future. For others, this change can be a painful time where relationships worsen and feelings of loss and sadness overwhelm. We can all agree that unthinkingly going through any significant life change without perspective, anticipation, or planning potentially increases the risk of adverse outcomes.

Because becoming an empty nester is a significant life change, it needs your focus, commitment, and energy. Fortunately, you can decide, define, and drive your best Empty Nest future. The following chapters will explore the research, pitfalls, and positive ways to embrace change and your Empty Nest journey. You should also note that this book is not a passive read. There will be data to consume, exercises to complete, and plans to be made. You won't be doing this alone. I will be with you each step to ensure you get the most out of the examples, content, investment, and time.

The Book's Origin

We live in a world where no one can definitively say they are the foremost authority on any subject. As Malcolm Gladwell discussed in his bestseller, *Outliers*, "To become an expert in something it takes roughly 10,000 hours." I would not be so bold as to claim I am the authority on empty nesting by authoring two books on the subject or experiencing it myself. When I started diving into this topic before becoming an empty nester, I quickly realized all the content was scattered and isolated. I found Empty Nest specific research and papers very narrowly focused, such as "Getting Kids Through College, Single-Parent Families Are Not All the Same." I found magazine articles on topics like "Investing as an empty nester" or tangential stories like "How to pack for your child when they go to college." I read through endless blogs and numerous posts that give helpful hints or state the top five ways to be an empty nester. To my amazement, everything about being an empty nester, let alone a single empty nester, was dispersed, generic, and sparse.

I was surprised that similar topics, such as childbirth, were rich with detailed examples and information. Books like *The Girlfriends Guide to Pregnancy*, *What to Expect When You Are Expecting*, and *The Expectant Father* have become required reading for any future mother, father, or parent. These books are fantastic because they are full of knowledge, anticipate questions, and help parents prepare for pregnancy and parenting. When I tried to find the equivalent for my upcoming Empty Nest status, I found that there wasn't a reader-friendly, comprehensive guide, how-to, or handbook on this topic. This was my motivation for the Empty Nest books.

In this book, I have summarized the themes and recommendations I have collected from over a hundred articles and research papers authored by counselors, psychologists, and academics. Additionally, I have attempted to distill all the good found in posts, forums, and blogs. Beyond reading every article I could find, I have had numerous conversations with pre-, current, and post-Empty Nest single parents. Now might be a good time to apologize to everyone I cornered at a party or pleaded to take my survey to gain knowledge on this topic. This book distills all the literature, posts, and real-world experiences I have uncovered. It includes insights from conversations, emotions, struggles, and successes that different people have encountered as they navigated through their single-parent Empty Nest journey.

As a parent of three, I have experienced the slow process of becoming an empty nester as each of my children left the house. Although the last child's departure makes the parent a certified empty nester, there are impacts and emotions when any child leaves the home. My fear led me to explore this topic, which I will explain later in this chapter. Fear led to obsession, and my obsession quickly became a personal mission not to fall into the negative scenarios I had uncovered on the subject and witnessed friends and peers who made this transition before me.

As my dive into this topic became more extensive, I realized my spouse, my friends, and all parents shifting to an Empty Nest status could benefit from what I uncovered. Sharing what I have learned, experienced, and put into practice became a driving force to how I could help others on their Empty Nest journey.

"Raising your child well is hard.
But learning to let them go out into
the world and prove that you did
your job right is even tougher."

—J. CRAINE

How It Started

This whole idea started with fear. As my children entered high school, I began contemplating my children's departure from home. Although this is viewed as an expected joyous time in any parent's life, I reflected on the state of my relationships. The more I thought about my active parenting and daily routine, the more I realized I was living an extremely family-focused agenda. Although family-focused sounds excellent on the surface, my daily interactions that weren't focused on work seemed to revolve entirely around my children—the nearly two decades of effort, care, and concentration I put into raising my three children had eclipsed all other relationships, goals, and self-exploration. My adult life seemed overshadowed by being a great parent. I became fearful and perhaps aware that this focus came at the expense of many other things.

You know the feeling after you buy a car, let's say a red Subaru, and you start noticing every other vehicle on the road seems to be a red Subaru? This is called frequency illusion, also known as the Baader–Meinhof phenomenon or frequency bias. Essentially, it is the tendency to notice something more often after seeing it for the first time. This leads to the person believing more red Subarus are on the road after buying a red Subaru. As I became more aware and concerned about my upcoming Empty Nest transition, I increasingly noticed couples and single parents a few years ahead of me, both at work and in our friend groups, struggling with their Empty Nest transition.

Each was at a point where their last child was going to college, and they seemed to be reevaluating their lives. I heard stories of anticipated sadness, fear, and uneasiness about their future. For the couples I spoke with, their married lives seemed to be in jeopardy or unraveling. Single parents were terrified of their purpose changing from an active parent to the unknown. With each confession, I became increasingly concerned about the unknown path in front of me. Although my Empty Nest timeline was still a few years away, I was scared.

The astounding thing about becoming an empty nester is that it is supposed to be a good thing. It's a time when a parent finally gets to enjoy themselves after raising their children. It is built up as a life milestone that represents freedom—a time when you can jump in your red Subaru and enjoy the world without the burden of raising a child. Red Subaru aside, what I thought this phase in my life should be versus the relationship reckoning I saw around me was alarming and concerning. The favorable Empty Nest scenario of freedom and celebration didn't play out in the stories I heard. I witnessed friends and colleagues struggle. I saw stress, sadness, and relationship flair-ups. I witnessed couples go their separate ways while single friends dealt with depression now that the goal of raising their child was complete. This realization hit me hard.

I have never been one to fear the unknown, but my expectations of a glorious Empty Nest future seemed uncertain for the first time. I wish I could tell you that my motivation for exploring this topic originated as something positive, but it didn't. My initial interest in this topic, which led to years of contemplating, planning, and working toward a solution, was not academic, charitable, or an exercise in learning; it was one hundred percent fear-based. I didn't want to fall into the same trap and experience the same negative results as those parents around me. With this realization, I was determined to face my fear.

Michelle's Single-Parent Journey

Michelle and her then-spouse David had Emma at age thirty. By Emma's fifth birthday, Michelle was a single parent, and David was out of the picture. Michelle's summary of raising Emma for the last thirteen years was put into three words, "It wasn't easy." Michelle is a self-described solo parent, breadwinner, and constant cheerleader. "There have been countless moments of fear and isolation, often regarding decisions I've had to make on my own." However, Michelle states, "Emma has been both my focus and anchor." "The hardest struggles?" Michelle repeated my question, "Financially, it has been a marathon, juggling saving for the future while trying to make ends meet. I have had to say no countless times to small requests, be it new clothes or a concert ticket I couldn't afford." But the hardest struggle, she confides, was the loneliness. "No partner to share victories, worries, late-night anxieties... that's a burden all single parents carry."

Despite the single-parent challenges Amy discussed, their mother-daughter bond seemed to thrive. "The beauty of our relationship, it's hard to describe. We built this life together; just as I am hers, she is my confidante, cheerleader, and partner in crime. We laugh and sometimes get into it, but we also dream together. It's a connection deeper than words." Now, with college decisions looming, their past routine hums in a different frequency. "Letting go? That's the ultimate test," Michelle admits.

On discussing Emma's departure, "College? I'm thrilled Emma will be going off to college. I mean, who wouldn't be? I'm bursting with pride, watching her blossom into this incredible young woman, knowing I helped her get to where she is today. But all the pride also contains bittersweet dread. Sure, let's not sugarcoat it—the thought of the Empty Nest next fall? It gives me hives. Quiet mornings alone, missing her face and her hugs… it's a whole new ball game, one I haven't even practiced for. But here's the thing: Emma's smart, driven, and ready. And as much as it scares me, I know I have to let her go. The truth is, I'm scared as hell, too. It's terrifying, yeah, but I wouldn't trade this journey for anything. I look at her, this strong, independent woman I raised, and I now have to be as strong in taking my own leap of faith into the unknown."

We're In The Same Boat

Michelle's interview left me both emotional and inspired. Although unique in its details, Michelle's worry and excitement about Emma leaving paralleled many of the sentiments I heard from other single parents. Michelle's positive attitude represents most parents I surveyed with a combination of love, pride, and excitement about their child's next chapter. But Michelle also clearly exemplifies the inner turmoil, sadness, and anxiety of the transition to empty nesting. My experience may differ from Michelle's, but on an emotional level, we had the same trepidation about what lies ahead. When I asked single-parent empty nesters, "Are you/were you looking forward to becoming an empty nester?" I received the following results:

Are you looking forward to becoming an empty nester?

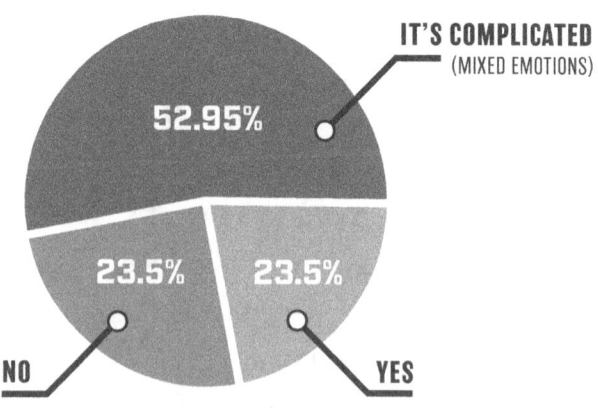

IT'S COMPLICATED
(MIXED EMOTIONS)

52.95%

23.5%   23.5%

NO   YES

This chart sums up the Empty Nest realization perfectly. Roughly 24 percent of single empty nesters look forward to this change while 24 percent do not. As for about 53 percent of single parents surveyed, it's complicated—there are no easy answers. In the next chapter, "The Average Single empty nester," we will dive further into the single-parent empty nester profile and discover the universality of this life change. These discoveries and examples can be both positive and negative, but as a whole, they are worthwhile in that they will help you become more self-aware of your Empty Nest journey.

CHAPTER 1 KEY POINTS

- Becoming an empty nester is a significant life change, not just a label.

- Most people don't prepare for an Empty Nest stage in life.

- Relationships between a parent and child, one's sense of self, and understanding of one's future are evaluated, redefined, and vulnerable during an Empty Nest transition.

- Becoming an empty nester requires focus, commitment, and energy to build your desired future.

"If you want to know what it feels like to be all things to all people, try being a single parent for a day."

The Average Single Empty Nester

The Empty Nest Profile

WHAT IS THE typical single empty nester profile? The quick answer is easy. It is a parent who has lived with a child and is now living alone, as their child has departed the home.

From a relationship status or parenting perspective, no single-parent Empty Nest profile exists. Being an empty nester

crosses multiple relationships at various stages. For example, an empty nester could be a single mom, dad, or guardian. It could include a multi-generational household with the parents and grandparents living under the same roof or a widower or widow raising a child independently. The commonality of each profile is one where a parent adjusts to life once their child leaves the home. To spare you a lot of repetition and time throughout this book, I will refrain from stating every conceivable person or relationship definition, every different type of parent, or every unique cohabitation relationship each time I reference a single-parent empty nester. From this point forward, I will refer to you or an empty nester as a single parent whose child will be leaving or has left the home.

To avoid repetitiveness, I will use eighteen years as the default age when a child leaves the home. Additionally, I will refer to the child going to college as the default reason they are leaving. If your child is leaving to join the military or to strike out on their own, or if they are twenty-three years old, please apply your circumstance. At times, I may focus on a once-married now single parent or discuss pregnancy as a typical Empty Nest experience. Again, if your relationship status or personal definition of single or parent doesn't fit into this profile, I ask that you substitute your own. Furthermore, unless stated otherwise, socially and geographically, the Empty Nest data and profiles I refer to throughout the book reside in the United States. This book was written for any person's parental or relationship situation; therefore, you should still be able to reflect, process, and embrace the actions, exercises, and solutions, as they are relative to all single parents.

As we move on to the next section, titled "The Numbers," I want to give you a fair warning that this section, more than any other section in the book, contains a lot of statistics. Much of the data here is harvested from surveys targeting single parents and empty nesters. If you aren't into numbers, consider the percentages as nothing more than data points where you can evaluate your thoughts and feelings and compare them to the average empty nester repeatedly quoted. I one hundred percent guarantee you will learn something. See how I just weaved in the first statistic?

The Numbers

Let's examine the average single empty nester in the United States. We can divide this topic into two parts: demographics and finances.

Demographics

According to the 2020 US Census, there are 22.5 million empty nesters in America. The majority are married, but this statistic includes second and third marriages. From a marital perspective, about 25 percent to 30 percent of all empty nesters are divorced. This statistic is increasing rapidly as the phenomenon of "gray divorces" grows. According to a 2021 Centers for Disease Control and Prevention (CDC) survey, one in three divorces in America are filed by couples over fifty-five years old. However, divorce alone is not the only reason an Empty Nest parent may be single. These numbers include parents who have never been married, single-parent adoptions, and parents who became widows or widowers.

To understand the average single Empty Nest in the United States, we must examine the different kinds of one-parent family groups.

MARITAL STATUS OF ONE-PARENT FAMILY GROUPS: 2022

US Census Bureau: 2022 Current Population Survey

MARITAL STATUS	MOTHERS	FATHERS
Single (never married)	51%	41%
Single (divorced)	29%	38%
Separated	16%	16%
Widowed	4%	5%

According to Statista's 2023 report, "Number of U.S. children living in a single parent family 1970-2023," 18.14 million children under the age of eighteen in 2023 lived in a single-parent household. 15.09 million children live with a single mother, and 3.05 million live with a single father. Perhaps surprisingly, half of all children in the US live with a single parent. Roughly 44 percent of children in a single-parent household live with a sibling. On a percentage basis, 80 percent of one-parent family groups lived with the mother. All this statistical data shows that single parents in the United States skew toward females.

Looking at the demographics of one-parent families, we can get a more detailed picture of the family makeup.

ONE-PARENT FAMILY GROUPS: 2022
US Census Bureau: 2022 Current Population Survey
ONE-PARENT FAMILY DEMOGRAPHICS
1970: 8.2 million One-Parent Families
2022: 18.14 million One-Parent Families
In 2022, 44% have two or more children under 18 in the home.
In 2022, 67% have one child under 12 years old.
In 2022, 51% of the population will have one child between 12 and 17 years old.

Although the difference between one-parent families from 1970 to 2022 has risen sharply, the Statista report notes, "Over the past decade, the share of families with children under 18, whether married couples or single parents, has stayed primarily steady." The data shows that the number of one-parent families has been roughly consistent for the past twenty-five years. Because of this, we can derive that the number of single empty nesting parents has remained constant in the US as parents fall into and age out of this period.

The average empty nester age range spans over twenty years, from forty-five to sixty-five. There are undoubtedly outliers on either end of the range, from teen mothers to second or third marriages that produce children later in life. Still, we will stick with the US Census definition for simplicity's sake.

Over time, the twenty-year empty nester span has been getting older and increasing due to changes in people's decision to have children. Most of the younger generation is waiting longer to get married, which impacts when they will have children. In 2021, according to the US Census Bureau, the average age of first marriage has significantly risen yearly to twenty-eight years old for women and thirty years old for men. Because of this, the age at which people have children is trending later, so the average age of an empty nester will continue to increase.

Two other factors have increased the age range of empty nesters. According to the CDC, there has been a sharp decline in teen pregnancies over the last thirty years. Additionally, the 2020 US Census data shows more people have children during a second or third marriage. This second and third go at having a family extends the Empty Nest timeline and age averages. Let's look at the average empty nester profile in the United States.

THE AVERAGE SINGLE EMPTY NESTER Taken from the 2020 US Census and the Bureau of Labor Statistics 2022	
The Median Age	51 years old (the average age of a parent when their last child leaves the house)
Education	90% have a high school diploma
	39% to over 50% have a college degree (the number varies by source)
Home Ownership	35% of single parents own a home (74% of married couples)
	Most empty nesters (single and married) are still in the process of paying down their mortgage.
Employment	76.9% of mothers in a single household are employed
	88.4% of fathers in a single household are employed

Finances

Although the average person becomes an empty nester at fifty-one, they will continue to work for at least ten more years. According to the Social Security Administration, the average retirement age in the US is sixty-four years old, with the average retirement age across all fifty states spanning from sixty-one to sixty-seven years old. Since retirement is still more than a decade out for most empty nesters, how much money has the average empty nester saved? According to Vanguard's "How America Saves 2022" report, the average forty-nine to fifty-four-year-old in the United States has saved $179,000 for retirement. It's important to note that the average is calculated by accounting for all people, adding all their savings up, and then dividing by the number of people. The average includes Jeff Bezos, Bill Gates, and Elon Musk. By the way, each of those three men is currently or will be an empty nester in the future.

If these numbers seem high, let's look at the median retirement savings for an empty nester. When we look at this number in Vanguard's report, the retirement savings decrease significantly to $61,500 for an individual.

The Average Single Empty Nester (Post High School Costs)

Beyond retirement savings, let's look at what the average single empty nester is saving for. Many parents who will become future empty nesters save money for their child's college expenses. According to the Fidelity Investments 2022 College Savings Indicator report, 76 percent of parents have started saving for college in 2022 versus just 58 percent of parents surveyed in 2007. That's an increase of 18 percent over fifteen years. Interestingly, the report states that saving for college is the number-one priority for a parent, followed by retirement, emergency funds, house/mortgage payments, and paying off credit card debt. "61.8% of recent high school graduates enrolled in college in October 2021," according to the Bureau of Labor Statistics, US Department of Labor.

A concerning Empty Nest statistic is that, according to Merrill Lynch's 2020 report, a parent, on average, will spend twice as much supporting their adult children as they contribute to their retirement account over the Empty Nest period. We can throw out the assumption that financial support for children stops when children leave home and there are fewer expenses associated with their departure. The statistics prove otherwise. According to the Merrill Lynch report, "79% of parents of early adults provide them with some type of financial support." The total amount of money spent by empty nesters on their adult children in the US totals a staggering $500 billion.

A 2021 report by Mintel states that a parent's spending habits don't change after a child leaves the home. This could be because the average empty nester is still working at this age, and their routine, spending habits, and mortgage payments or rent stay consistent. Although the household cost of food and utilities may decrease when a child leaves the home, according to the Mintel Report, a parent's lifestyle remains constant.

Let's look at the average empty nester's income and spending.

THE AVERAGE SINGLE EMPTY NESTER SPEND Source: Merrill Lynch's 2020 report & US Census data & The Bureau of Labor Statistics	
Salary	$76,214 a year
Income	$60,000 a year
Continued Spend	Average credit card debt: $3,503.57 (2020)
	Median monthly mortgage payment: $1,775 (2022) Median monthly rent: $1,372 (2023)
	$254 is the average monthly spend on supporting a child who has left the home ($3,048 annually) This equates to 5% of a single-parent's income.

If the average empty nester spends $254 monthly on their adult children, what specifically are they subsidizing? Monthly cell phone costs and rent are the top two fully subsidized expenses. The top partial subsidy is food and groceries. Here is a more complete breakdown.

How Parents support their adult children (18-34)

The Financial Journey of Modern Parenting. (2023, March 8). Merrill Lynch.

	Some support	Pay In Full
Cell phone	22%	32%
Rent/Mortgage	13%	32%
Student Loans	18%	27%

Food & Groceries	37%	23%
School	22%	22%
Vacations	23%	21%
Car Expenses	30%	17%

Now that you know what the average empty nester is subsidizing, let's look at how they pay these expenses.

How parents pay to support their adult children (oldest child 18+)

The Financial Journey of Modern Parenting. (2023, March 8). Merrill Lynch.

Pull money from savings	50%
Live a less comfortable lifestyle	43%
Take on debt	26%
Pull money from a retirement account	25%
Retire later/work longer	19%
Refinance home	14%
Come out of retirement	9%

Perhaps this is why no one has ever said raising a child is inexpensive. In a September 2023 report, Lending Tree projected that it costs the average parent or family in the US $237,482 over eighteen years to raise a child. That cost varied greatly by state. For example, the eighteen-year cost estimate to raise a child is highest in Hawaii at $314,529 and lowest in South Carolina at $169,327. Mind you, these numbers are for one child from birth to eighteen years old living under the same roof. If a parent continues to pay their child's expenses beyond eighteen, as the previous data suggests, costs can skyrocket with the addition of college tuition and separate living expenses.

We now understand an average empty nester's demographics, financials, and support spending habits. These numbers fluctuate considerably from household to household across the United States. These statistics aren't a call for action or personal judgment but rather a prompt where you can reflect on your demographic and financial state. Although numbers and statistics are interesting, they only tell part of the story. In the following two sections, I will summarize the average single empty nester's household profile and sentiment. Sentiment equates to the concerns and thoughts of the average empty nester toward their children and how they feel about their newfound status.

Household Dynamics and Communication

As parents aged forty-five to sixty-five launch their adult children into the world, many realize that their Empty Nest timeline may be more complex than they initially thought. Many adult children today are living with a parent longer or boomeranging back home after their initial launch, and trends in ongoing communication and contact with their parents continue to change.

There is a lot of interesting data about household dynamics and the average empty nester's expectations concerning their children. I have summarized some of the critical parental sentiments and statistics in the following table.

THE AVERAGE EMPTY NEST HOUSEHOLD
2019 survey of 1,860 empty nesters by 55Places.com

21 years old was the average age at which children departed the house.

50% of parents stated their children lived with them longer than expected.

38% experienced one or more of their children moving back home.

58% think that their children will probably return home.

66% wouldn't mind if their children moved back home.

86% with adult children at home believe their children will be financially independent in the next two years.

The trend of adult children living with a parent for a more extended period in the United States is increasing. According to the US Census Bureau's 2021 America's Families and Living Arrangements report, more than one-half (58 percent) of adults ages eighteen to twenty-four lived in a parental home compared to 17 percent of adults ages twenty-five to thirty-four. The top four reasons supporting this change are:

1. Children attending college while at home
2. Unemployment in younger adults

3. Student loan debt
4. Children wanting financial stability before they leave home

The boomerang situation for empty nesters is not necessarily viewed as bad.

THE AVERAGE BOOMERANG EMPTY NEST HOUSEHOLD 2022 Neighbor.com survey, which consisted of over one thousand parents
57% said they would let their child move back home (no strings attached).
10% said they would charge rent.
11% would only let them move back in case of an emergency.
10% said their child could move back but only into an unused space, such as a spare room, basement, or garage.
6% would not let their child move back home.
86% with adult children at home believe their children will be financially independent in the next two years.

In the cases where the adult child doesn't move back home, it was reported that most adult children stayed close to home after they moved out. According to the survey, 56 percent of parents said their children remained within an hour's drive after leaving the family home. Another 12 percent said their children were less than three hours away. Regardless of physical proximity, 25 percent of empty nester parents stated they see their children multiple times per month while 24 percent only see their children a few times during the year.

According to the Mintel 2021 empty nester Marketing report, parents' top concerns regarding the communication and emotional aspects of children leaving the home center around their children's safety and the ongoing connection with them. What does that typical "ongoing connection" look like? The 55Places.com 2019 study pointed out that a parent still prefers to keep in touch regularly after their children leave, although how they do this and how often varies greatly.

THE AVERAGE EMPTY-NEST COMMUNICATION 2019 survey of 1,860 empty nesters by 55Places.com	
FREQUENCY	34% stated that they communicate with their children every day.
	41% keep in touch more than once per week.
	21% keep in contact with their child every month.
HOW	44% of parents call their children.
	33% text.
	12% prefer FaceTime.
CHANGE	42% say their communication with their child has decreased.
	30% said that they speak to their children more now.
	28% experienced no change.

We now understand why most empty nesters continue to pay for their children's cell phones.

The Personal Sentiment

How is the average empty nester doing? The answer to this question is complex and dynamic. For example, if we asked, "How are you doing? How is parenting? How is your career?" we would receive a variety of answers. These stages in life come with ups and downs, triumphs and struggles, good and bad. One can answer these questions after considering the totality of the period or how they feel now. Similar to the previous questions, there is no easy answer for single empty nesters, but we do have some data, and the data represents a problem.

> **"There is no easy answer for single empty nesters, but we do have some data, and the data represents a problem."**

When we asked a hundred single-parent empty nesters if they were currently or anticipate they would enjoy being an empty nester, the numbers continued to tell a mixed story: 53 percent said yes, 6 percent said no, and 41 percent had mixed emotions.

Are you currently enjoying or anticipate enjoying being an empty nester?

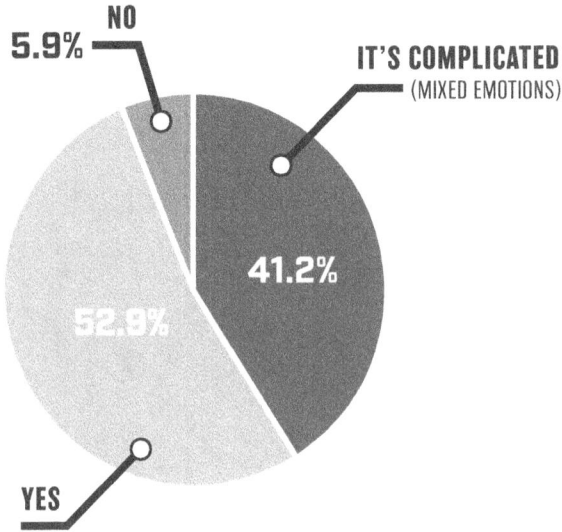

To understand this more thoroughly, we asked about the biggest concerns of the single-parent empty nester. The data shows that one's health, both physical and mental, is the primary concern. Tied for the second biggest concern was their child's "well-being and safety" and retirement.

What are/were your biggest concerns for single empty nesters? [Select all that apply]

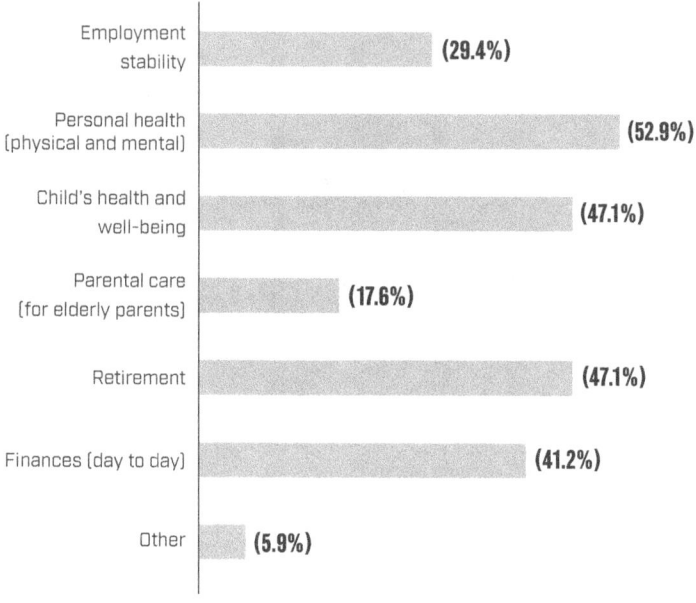

This data shows that an Empty Nest parent has multiple concerns. When surveyed about the positive aspects of becoming an empty nester, the answers varied greatly, from personal to pride, healing to routines. Here are some of the most representative responses to the question, "What are the positives as a soon-to-be or current single empty nest parent?":

- Seeing my daughter flourish.
- Anticipated freedom from daily routines, ability to pick and choose at-home activities, and opportunities to travel.

- Self-reflection and healing from a codependent relationship and feelings of failure at parenting.
- I can date again.
- Lowered expenses, more free time, and independent decision-making. I know my own day-to-day choices don't impact anyone other than myself.
- A clean house. Quiet. Independence that I haven't had in seventeen years of single parenting.
- I only have to worry about me.
- Pride in seeing my son's achievements and successes.

As the responses show, the sentiment of a single-parent empty nester is complicated, based on emotions and responsibilities. For this reason, a summary definition of sentiment is hard to define. You'll recall at the end of the last chapter, when we asked a hundred single-parent empty nester if they were looking forward to being an empty nesters, 24 percent looked forward to this change while 24 percent did not. The remaining 55 percent of single parents surveyed stated that it was complicated and that they had mixed emotions. I believe this statistic accurately tells the story.

Statistics Are Just Statistics

I like a quote by Ron DeLegge II in *Gents with No Cents*. DeLegge says, "99 percent of all statistics only tell 49 percent of the story." In this section, more than any other, I pulled together a lot of statistics and percentages. Although they are great for supporting a concept of what the average single-parent empty nester is like, Ron is right. The percentages only tell half the story. Here is the other side of the story:

- 48% of empty nesters aren't supporting their adult children.
- 43% wouldn't let their children move back home with no strings attached.
- 53% aren't concerned about retirement.
- 56% don't call their children.

These statements are all true, yet they paint a very different picture than I detailed in this chapter. For every statistic I quoted, there was a neutral or negative response not quoted. If 50 percent of empty nesters miss their children, we can assume the other 50 percent don't. Perhaps they don't have an opinion. I'm not sure which is worse.

After finishing this section, we can take it as a positive sign if you feel good about your Empty Nest status compared to the average empty nester. If you feel like there are some areas where you and your relationships can improve, that's okay, too. I expect the numbers we just went through to ground you just as they ground me. The average single-parent empty nester should give you some perspective on where you are and what's coming as you embark on your Empty Nest journey.

The average single empty nester will continue to have a lot of responsibilities after their children leave. They will continue to work, save for retirement, and have an adult-child relationship to foster along with their routine household responsibilities. The personal and emotional process of becoming an empty nester brings a lot of change. As we have seen in the data, it is a time of reflection on oneself and others while trying to understand their future wants and needs. As with any change, emotions and feelings are bound to be heightened. It is a vulnerable and deeply personal time for individuals. The average single-parent empty nester may not experience every emotion, but there is more and more data supporting that this transition can be a tricky one for us all.

My deep dive into this topic has given me a lot of information, but perhaps the biggest takeaway is that each of our Empty Nest journeys is unique. We are complex individuals with varied histories, experiences, emotions, and internal thoughts. In the end, comparing ourselves to the average single-parent empty nester is an exciting and informative exercise; however, none of us are average when we step back and examine the complexity of our journey through life.

In the next chapter, we will toss out the statistics and percentages and avoid quoting the average. It's time to focus on you, the empty nester.

CHAPTER 2 KEY POINTS

- There is a profile of the average single empty nester.

- The average single empty nester continues financially supporting their children after they leave the home.

- The average single empty nester has their health, their child's well-being, and financial concerns as top of mind.

- The average single empty nester has mixed emotions regarding this change in life.

"Nothing
you do for
children is
ever wasted."

— GARRISON KEILLOR

CHAPTER THREE

You, The Empty Nester

LET'S FIRST THINK through what your child will do at the start of your Empty Nest journey. Your child will be turning eighteen or edging closer to it. They will start to see themselves through another lens, an adult lens. Being eighteen signifies when a teen legally becomes an adult, but it can indicate the end of one's childhood. There is a lot to digest in that last sentence, but for efficiency's sake, we will move forward with your child's timeline. Their independence and self-esteem will grow as they graduate from high school, get into college, and get a full-time job. Although these milestones are steps toward your child's independence, the

acknowledgment and act of leaving home accelerates their growth, maturity, and personal responsibility. Put another way, this time of pre- and post-departure will probably be a monumental growth cycle for your child. When your child leaves your home, there is excessive time and effort dedicated to their departure: the planning, packing, readiness, and the physical move. Once the physical move happens, a significant milestone for them is accomplished: living without you. And your household changes forever.

Your child's departure is not all about them. From an empty nester's perspective, it's all about you. You become the empty nester. When your child leaves the home, your relationship with your child will change. You have been an active parent, but that will change. You have been a nesting family, and that will change. If it didn't happen already, you'll realize that your child is no longer a child. This means your parenting responsibility will change.

For the first time in literally years, you will find yourself on your own again, a single person under one roof. Adjusting to a new normal of a childless routine will become a time of introspection and reflection. Your happiness, your career, your sex life, your future, and your relationships with others may all be questioned. Becoming a single empty nester will shift your relationship with your child, where you will be faced with feelings of loss, joy, sadness, pride, and perhaps distress. You will reflect and reevaluate your sense of purpose, your passions, your future wants, and your relationships.

The realization you will face is that your active parenting years are over. To put it bluntly, the rest of your life will be one where you now focus on yourself. Please don't underestimate the importance or impact of this transition or you will leave yourself open to outcomes you may not want. More on this later.

So Now What?

Here you are, an empty nester. Yes, you are still a parent. Yes, you still have a child or children in this world, but they have left the nest. What does your empty nester life look like?

No one knows what it's like to be a parent until they become one. If I were to say, "I know what it's like to raise a child because I babysat children when I was a teenager," that would seem preposterous. Perhaps the same holds for becoming an empty nester. We learn by living and experiencing the moment. Whether being a freshman in high school, becoming a parent, or being an empty nester, you don't quite know what it would be like or how it would feel until you become that thing. This applies to almost any stage in life.

What kind of empty nester experience do you have? You likely have experienced glimpses of your empty nester life. Perhaps there was a time when your child was sleeping over at a friend's house for an evening. Maybe they went to camp or vacationed with a friend for a few days. On these rare occasions, you got a glimpse of having the house to yourself while you experienced the awkward feeling of waking up without your child present. Is this the feeling of being an empty nester? I think the answer is sort of.

As a parent of three, there weren't many occasions where all three of my children were out of the house overnight at the same time. When I experienced one of these rare evenings, I felt a sense of freedom and excitement. There was freedom to have a night off from parenting, from worrying about where your child was, what they were doing, or when they were coming home. Even more surprising, waking up without a child's itinerary seemed magical and liberating. But I also knew that this was a one-off feeling. I could rest assured that my children and my active parenting routine would recommence upon their return. I was far from understanding the impact of their more permanent absence.

As a parent, there are a few moments when you don't have to worry or concern yourself with your child. I always found it strange when my children were safe somewhere else. My experiences of childless freedom were short-lived. The evenings were more of a stay-cation versus a dry run of my Empty Nest future. Just as a five-day vacation in Hawaii is not the same as living in Hawaii for five years, my glimpse into an Empty Nest lifestyle was not a good test case for my life once my children left. Even on the exciting, accessible, magical, and liberating nights when my children were safely elsewhere, I often wondered what they were up to. Breaking away from my children for just one night wasn't that hard, but breaking away for a lifetime and transitioning to an empty nester is something else altogether.

Instead of wondering what your Empty Nest future will be like, perhaps a better question to ask ourselves is, "What kind of empty nester do you want to be?" To answer that question, you need to get some perspective on the experience, the process, and what others have faced. You must also understand the difficulties and greatness your Empty Nest journey can become. We are not giving up on answering any of the questions. Your exploration into this journey for answers has only just begun.

My Children's Departure

Every parent-child relationship is complex and different, just as every empty nester journey will be different. The majority of this book is focused on how to identify and prepare for your transition to becoming an empty nester. Beyond your journey, you have your relationship with your child. Although I went through the same physical experience when my children left the house, I experienced different reactions, feelings, and emotions when each child departed. In speaking to other empty nesters before me, not surprisingly, their experiences with their children were different than mine. I don't interpret these differences as good or bad; I now understand that they are uniquely our own.

Over your child's lifetime, you have built and fostered a unique relationship with them. You are a listener, a disciplinarian, a counselor, or a combination of a million roles based on your parenting style. There is no cookie-cutter parent-child relationship, regardless of whether you have ten children or one. Each relationship is highly personalized. With this in mind, your experience when your child leaves, including the months leading up to their departure, the departure day, and the months following, will be individualized to you. On the following pages, I'll share my and my children's departure journeys. I am sharing these experiences with you in the hope that they will provide context for your journey and other chapters in this book.

> **"There is no cookie-cutter parent-child relationship, regardless of whether you have ten children or one. Each relationship is highly personalized."**

The Build Up

My empty nester concern about the pending departure of my three children was not initially centered around their well-being or their transition to life on their own. The realization that my children would leave led me to examine how my life would change upon their departure. As you know, this led me to explore my relationships and dive into what empty nesting is. The children leaving was the cause of my empty nester concern, but it was not the initial focus. I was fearful that I hadn't focused or prepared for this next stage in life. Somewhat ironically, I believed I had focused and well-prepared my children for their next stage in life. Looking back, it seems a bit backward.

However, if we look at my Empty Nest timeline, my exploration of the topic spanned years, and each of my child's departure processes (pre and post) seemed to happen over a six-to-nine-month period. There is no value in worrying about your child leaving for college when they are a sophomore in high school. You still have three years of high school to worry about. However, preparing yourself for the upcoming empty nester phase made sense to me.

As college approached, I felt my children would survive and thrive independently. More than that, I was excited for them. Yes, I did have some concerns, which I will discuss later, but I was looking forward to them having new experiences, maturing, and becoming independent. As we have already established, you don't know what an experience is like until it happens to you. The only real experience I had around college departure was my own. Let's start there.

My Departure

Because I was the youngest child of four, my departure from home made my parents empty nesters. Honestly, I never thought about my parent's Empty Nest journey. Perhaps there is a lesson in this realization, or maybe it just underscores how seventeen- to twenty-year-olds can be pretty self-absorbed. I have no idea how much jubilation or sorrow they felt when I left, but my gut tells me it was more on the jubilation side. Then again, it was a different time when I went to school. Hyper-connected parenting didn't exist because there was no tracking whereabouts, instant communication, or ongoing academic progress reports. Once I left the house, my parents could not communicate with me besides the US Post Office or landline telephone. There were no drop-off days at college, cell phones, parent portals, or FaceTime. Additionally, my experience when leaving the house was quite different for my parents than it was for me as a parent. Most parents today, including myself, are much more aware of all aspects of their child's life and participate in the departure process versus just witnessing it.

My college departure consisted of very little preparation. I'd call it a "slam dunk" off to college experience. I rented a U-Haul with a friend. I packed up all my belongings into boxes, and I left. It was as simple as that. There was no IKEA trip, no "this is how you cook an egg," and no "make sure you register for classes." I remember waving goodbye to my parents standing in the driveway, and that was it. There was an "I'll see you at Thanksgiving" mindset that seemed generally accepted by my siblings and parents. Although my departure story may seem abrupt, it was probably expected. I grew up with an expectation of attending college. I grew up not expecting any college preparation or involvement from my parents. Applying to college, enrolling, and doing campus visits was something you did on your own. When it came to leaving, my parents didn't participate in pre-departure shopping, budgeting, or even packing. I was on my own both financially and organizationally.

My example is not to cast stones at my parents but rather to bring up that my Empty Nest departure was not a shared experience with my parents. It happened, but it mainly occurred in isolation. Introspectively, I transitioned out of the home on my own, and I did fine. My siblings transitioned out on their own and were fine. My wife did it on her own, and she was fine. This explains why I felt my children's transition would be relatively trouble-free and acknowledged that they had the additional benefit of help all along the way. This is an excellent example of one's own experience shaping their attitude, concerns, and perspective toward their child's experience.

As we all know, things are very different today when a child leaves the home. The advent of the cell phone alone, giving a parent or child the ability to call, text, FaceTime, or track the whereabouts of each other, creates a life of connectivity and communication that was not present in the past.

And the cell phone is just one example of hyper-connectivity, which we will explore deeper later in the book. On average, there is more involvement between parents and children today in planning, preparing, and driving the child's departure process than ever. Parents are more involved and spend more time with their children than they did in the past. I know I promised earlier to spare you more statistics, but to support this point, researchers at the University of California, Irvine, found that between 1965 and 2012, ten Western nations showed an increase in the amount of time parents spent with their children.

- In 1965, single mothers spent an average of forty-three minutes on childcare activities.
- In 2012, single mothers spent an average of a hundred and one minutes on childcare activities.

A father's time with children nearly quadrupled.

- In 1965, dads spent a daily average of just sixteen minutes with their children.
- In 2012, fathers spent about fifty-nine minutes a day caring for them.

In June 2023, the US Bureau of Labor Statistics released the 2022 American Time Use Survey. This report showed that Adults with children under age six spent an average of 2.1 hours per day providing primary childcare to household children. These are significantly higher numbers than the 2012 data. Regardless of whether these numbers seem high or low, parents today, on average, spend more time with their children than they did in the past.

Regarding my departure, my parents did their best and followed the path that felt right to them then. Your parents probably did the same. As for your child's departure journey, I have a sneaky suspicion you have been or will be "all in" and actively part of the process compared to how your departure went. Let's now turn to what your child is doing as they prepare to leave.

The Nostalgic and the Disengaged

There are many articles on how a teen feels when going to college. If you google that sentence, you will find over one billion results. Most articles quote that teens will have some anxiety, nervousness, and fear about college. They state that teens will want to fit in, don't know what to expect academically, and worry that college life may not be what they expected.

Instead of going down that research tangent and repeating what you can find yourself, let me share my theory of the two emotional groups teens fall into when departing their homes. This is based on my experience and what I have observed and discussed with other parents as their teens ramped up for departure. I believe there are two prevalent groups most teens fall into during the days leading up to their departure: the Nostalgic and the Disengaged teen.

The Nostalgic teen embraces their pre-departure days, usually in the summer leading up to college, with their friends and family.

The Nostalgic teen is excited about their transition and independence yet wishes to be with and bond with their parents, family, and friends before time runs out. Although all college-bound teens have some anxiety and nervousness, the Nostalgic teen is more likely to feel optimistic about their current home. They are determined to make the most of their time before leaving. The Nostalgic teen wants to leave the house with a solid parent-child relationship and lock in all their relationships. The Nostalgic teen comes across as confident in their interactions with family and may know how their parents will feel once they leave.

The Disengaged teen anticipates their pending departure as more of a breakup from their parents, friends, and home.

I believe this is a standard defense mechanism that happens subconsciously. The Disengaged teen usually starts flexing their independence and tries to reduce their reliance on their parents, gradually leading up to their final departure. This flexing can include testing and pushing boundaries, a more contentious attitude toward their parents, and becoming more distant from family and friends. The overall attitude of a Disengaged teen is "I can't wait to leave." I want to point out that the Disengaged teen isn't bad or negative; they are just coping with the upcoming change differently.

If given a choice, we would all choose Nostalgic for our departing teens. Departing from home is a big emotional step for a child. How they process that departure shouldn't be judged based on the fact that processing itself is healthy. The reality is that many teens going through the pre-departure process will probably sit somewhere in the middle of the Nostalgia and Disengaged examples. Most teens probably have flare-ups of disengagement, followed by moments of nostalgia. Most teens have moments of connection before they leave, but they may also test boundaries and independence. Your teen may fit into one category more than the other, but they likely share both traits.

I shared my theory with you because it will provide a pretext for my children's three departures and perhaps help you understand your child's feelings about departure. I also hope that you will realize that if your child has more disengaged teen characteristics, you will have more understanding and empathy that they are just coping with change. If you can, focus on the positives and don't take the bumps in the departure timeline personally. For the record, when I left home, I was a disengaged teen. I pushed boundaries, cut ties with high school friends, and couldn't wait to leave. I'm sure my parents felt jubilation because of my actions leading up to my departure.

My Goodbyes (Physical and Emotional)

To say I was involved in the departures of our three children going off to college would be an understatement. I became actively engaged years before when SAT and ACT preparation began. From that point on, I was involved in the college application process, including touring schools and ramping up for their college transition before they left. I was so emotionally invested in the process that, when each child didn't get into a school, I felt rejected, and when they were admitted into a college, it felt as if I accomplished that feat as well. I'll discuss this later in the book, but I was a helicopter parent.

After high school graduation, the summer before my children went to college, I made packing checklists, created a "what do you need in your dorm" inventory, and took trips to IKEA and Target to ensure they were set for college living. I read up on college move-in day procedures and planned each drop-off trip to their schools. On drop-off day, I hauled boxes, helped set up rooms, and did some initial grocery shopping to ensure their transition into a new space was comfortable and complete. My children's journey out of the nest was a shared experience with each of my children.

My experience with my first and second child was similar. My son and daughter intensely looked forward to attending college and flexing their independence. They were each more Nostalgic than Disengaged, but in the days leading up to their departures, there were moments of pushback and heightened emotions as they tested their independence with their mother and me. As a former Disengaged, I realized this was a natural separation anxiety action and likely a self-defense mechanism. There was still a little more head-butting than I would have liked. In hindsight, I, too, was going through a transition of letting go. As a self-proclaimed helicopter parent, it's entirely possible that I was testing the boundaries of my control while they were asserting their own. By the end of their pre-departure summer, I was ready for their drop-off day. They were equally prepared to stretch their wings and leave the nest. In a way, the timing worked out perfectly for me and my first two children.

> **"as a self-proclaimed helicopter parent, it's entirely possible that I was testing the boundaries of my control while they were asserting their own."**

For my wife, the departure of our first child seemed more complicated. Her pre-departure feelings were more nostalgic, and I believe the mother/son and first child bond had something to do with it. She was excited for him but also experienced sadness in the anticipation of missing him. There was no head-butting or alpha male testing between my son and his mother. Their departure journeys for each other were Nostalgic. When our second child left, our eldest daughter, the departure seemed more manageable for my wife. I believe the process with our son set emotional expectations, and I recall there was a bit of the mother-daughter disengagement dynamic at work. Maybe alpha female tension? The departures, move-in days, and overall sentiment were well received by our first two children, but each of our emotional journeys as parents differed.

When our last child left, our youngest daughter, I had mixed emotions. I was excited for her to go, and she was excited about leaving. By this time, I had relinquished most of the control issues that I experienced with my first two children. This meant I was in a better place. I felt confident in my upcoming household existence because I had already created my Empty Nest Blueprint (more on this in chapter 13). I was pretty comfortable with the forthcoming change; everything seemed nostalgic. However, in my mind, I knew this was the big one. This was the final departure that would literately make me an empty nester. I knew that, with this departure, a more dramatic shift in my life was coming, and I realized that I had become accustomed to a predictable household with my daughter in it. Emotionally, this departure was more challenging for me than the first two because it was the last child leaving. Perhaps this was the last gasp of a father and young daughter relationship before all of my children turned into adults. Again, the temperament of our household was Nostalgic, but this departure represented the finality of the daily parenting routine I had been practicing for the last twenty-two years. My Empty Nest status was happening.

After They Left

After each child's departure, I had ah-ha moments of realization that they were gone. Understandably, there were moments of missing them. These realizations and moments came with little flashes of sadness. This didn't happen when I passed their empty bedroom or saw their high school graduation picture on the mantel. I had these moments when I thought of something I wanted to share with them, only to realize they were not around. The thoughts were usually just random things like a movie recommendation or a funny moment in my day that I knew they would like. At times, these fleeting moments didn't seem worth an interruption (text or call), so the feeling of their absence was all the more present.

In hindsight, I realize I could have quickly texted or called them, and perhaps other parents in that situation would have. Philosophically, I decided that, when each of my children left, I should give them as much space as possible and allow them to reach out when they wanted to connect. The joke I want to tell, a movie I want to discuss, or the thought I just had might be something they would enjoy, but reaching out every moment I tried to connect seemed like an intrusion. You can see once again how my experience with my parents dictated my connection philosophy. I made a decision, and

I felt comfortable letting them go and giving them space and time to develop their routine of independence without daily updates or my problem-solving for them. Even with all my Empty Nest research, preparations, and plans, it was still an adjustment.

Beyond missing my children after they left, the other persistent feeling I experienced was wondering if they were safe or okay. Since your child was a newborn baby, many of your actions as a parent have been to keep your child safe and protected. Where are they? What are they doing? And are they okay? All parents knowingly or unconsciously think about these three questions over and over while raising a child. We have been doing this for a child's entire lifetime. This, for me, was a hard habit to break. For some odd reason, these protective thoughts would come to me late at night or on weekends. I realized my worry emerged because I assumed nights and weekends equate to being out and about, and I hoped they were using their best judgment. Again, my philosophy of letting go of control and letting them grow initially trumped my taking action to check in and see if they were okay late at night. In full disclosure, I would, at times, check "find my friends" to see if they were near their dorm or apartment, but this is somewhat meaningless data other than to rule out interstate kidnapping.

Overall, one of the big positives I had in my corner is something you will have after this book. I felt my children were prepared to leave. I also felt ready to adjust to my children leaving the home with the research and knowledge I had gained. I was aware an upcoming pre-departure Empty Nest stage existed, and I had a perspective of the pitfalls, emotions, and outcomes of what an Empty Nest journey entails.

In the next chapter, we move away from focusing on the empty nester profile to understand a phenomenon called Empty Nest Syndrome.

CHAPTER 3 KEY POINTS

🖋 Your child's departure is not only about them; it is also about you.

🖋 Parents today are more involved with their children leaving the nest than ever.

🖋 Your departing child may be Nostalgic (embracing their relationships before they leave).

🖋 Your child may be Disengaged (testing boundaries and "breaking up" with relationships before they leave).

🖋 When your child departs, it is an emotional and physical journey.

"There are two times when parenting is the most difficult. When the baby arrives home, the adult first leaves home."

—JENNIFER QUINN

CHAPTER FOUR

Empty Nest Syndrome

Empty Nest Syndrome

EMPTY NEST SYNDROME is not a disease, a virus, or something you can catch from someone else. It's not considered a medical condition or a psychiatric diagnosis. Just because it doesn't carry a medical diagnosis doesn't mean it isn't a major emotional transitional phase that one shouldn't prepare for and be aware of. Mayo Clinic states, "Empty Nest Syndrome is a phenomenon where parents experience feelings of sadness

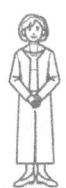

and loss when the last child leaves home." *Psychology Today* defines Empty Nest Syndrome as "The distress and other complicated emotions that parents often experience when their children leave home." Compounded with feelings of loss, sadness, and distress, Empty Nest Syndrome can further cause emotional hardship to an individual. For example, experiencing Empty Nest Syndrome can affect one's sense of self and their evolving relationship with their child, and it can make one recognize that they are entering a new phase of their life on their own.

If Empty Nest Syndrome had a definition sibling, one could compare it to a cross between the "baby blues" and postpartum depression (PPD). The Mayo Clinic says, "Most new moms experience postpartum "baby blues" after childbirth, which commonly includes mood swings, crying spells, anxiety, and difficulty sleeping. The baby blues usually begin within the first two to three days after delivery and may last up to two weeks." When these feelings are more severe and longer lasting, they can lead to postpostpartum depression. WebMD defines postpartum depression as "A complex mix of physical, emotional, and behavioral changes that happen in some women after giving birth." Having baby blues is not a medical condition or a clinical diagnosis, whereas postpartum depression is.

There are many similarities between these two experiences and Empty Nest Syndrome. All three deal with depression, sadness, loss of a sense of self, and worry about a new role (motherhood/empty nester). Much like Empty Nest

Syndrome, this phenomenon is not limited to only females. Mayo Clinic states, "Studies show that new fathers can experience postpartum depression, too. They may feel sad, tired, overwhelmed, anxious, or have changes in their usual eating and sleeping patterns. These are the same symptoms that mothers with postpartum depression experience."

The period of Empty Nest Syndrome also parallels our two childbirth examples. According to the *Harvard Review of Psychiatry*, a 2014 review of studies suggests that "PPD symptoms improve over time, with many cases of depression resolving three to six months after they begin." A similar timeline exists for Empty Nest Syndrome. For the majority of people, feelings of loss and depression when their child leaves can last a few days or weeks, and like PPD, in more severe cases, it can last much longer.

Empty Nest Syndrome can be as simple as a parent adjusting to their child leaving the nest, or it can encompass a litany of much greater life struggles with relationships. For example, signs of Empty Nest Syndrome beyond sadness and loss include individuals struggling with their sense of self and purpose, questioning their relationships, and struggling with their new role as parents. This is much more than just missing your child after they have moved out.

Empty Nest Syndrome can be as simple as a parent adjusting to their child leaving the nest, or it can encompass a litany of much greater life struggles with relationships.

Recognizing that Empty Nest Syndrome exists and understanding its signs and struggles allows you to discover solutions, avoid adverse outcomes, and be empathetic and knowledgeable to others in the same situation (including your children).

Predisposition

While numerous variables can predispose parents to Empty Nest Syndrome, some relationship dynamics are riskier. *Psychology Today* states, "Women normally suffer more than men do, and feelings of sadness may be more pronounced among stay-at-home parents whose lives were organized around meeting the everyday needs of their children." Adding to this example, a parent hyper-involved in their children's lives, activities, and social circles may experience a more significant loss when those activities cease. It goes without question that a single parent who is the sole parental figure with the primary nurturing relationship with their child would be impacted to a much greater degree. In this case, separation anxiety and a sense of loss of connection can be more significant. A single parent or a full-time parent tends to be more susceptible to Empty Nest Syndrome.

Being an involved parent or having a close relationship implies you have a rewarding and fulfilling bond as a parent. The only cause for concern is that the closer the parent-child relationship is, the more significant the emotional impact of the child's departure from the home may be.

Contributing Factors / Parallel Issues

Beyond the parent-child relationship, additional internal factors add to Empty Nest Syndrome. For example, a person who may be more isolated and not have a strong support group of friends, peers, or family may find themselves with an increased feeling of sadness and depression. The stress and vulnerability of an Empty Nest transition can add to isolation and potentially lead to it.

Whether one works or not does not necessarily build a safety net preventing Empty Nest Syndrome. A single parent who works full-time is inevitably balancing career stresses in addition to parenting at home. Layer the emotional toll of Empty Nest Syndrome on top of an already full plate of priorities and responsibilities, and one can see how stress and negative emotions can fester and grow. Conversely, a single parent who doesn't work and whose sense of purpose and identity has revolved around raising their children would be equally susceptible to Empty Nest Syndrome. When one's identity and sense of purpose are changed or abruptly end (i.e., when a child moves out), that missing piece of self-worth can be debilitating.

There is no perfect time for a child to leave your home, and unfortunately, in the Empty Nest phase of our lives, a variety of outside factors can likely add to the stress and anxiety of the situation.

As we covered previously, the average empty nester is between forty-four and sixty-five. During this period, it is typical for a series of additional stressful life events and challenges to occur. The following life events can magnify and increase the symptoms of Empty Nest Syndrome.

- Loss of a parent
- Losing, plateauing, or changing jobs
- Pressure associated with downsizing or the relocation of one's home
- Midlife crisis
- Menopause
- Retirement and financial pressures
- Responsibilities and care of an elderly parent

Research suggests that Empty Nest Syndrome can cause sadness, a sense of purposelessness, and feelings of rejection. In the article "The Empty Nest Syndrome: Myth or Reality?" Jana L. Raup and Jane E. Myers state that parents' "concern for the welfare of adult children... may contribute to feelings of anxiety, worry, and stress." Parents frequently wonder if they have done enough to prepare their children to live independently and safely. These feelings of anxiety and concern can easily spill over into the parent-child relationship.

When a child leaves the home, it is easy for a parent to default to and focus solely on the departing child. Often, they have not considered their emotional future. Being otherwise distracted, they may leave themselves open to a floodgate moment of complex emotions, where Empty Nest Syndrome arises. Empty Nest Syndrome itself can be a challenge, but when you add the internal and external pressures of these life events, it is understandable how overwhelming this transition can be.

The Key Takeaway

Empty Nest Syndrome is a natural and emotional phenomenon affecting many people during the Empty Nest transition and the parent-child relationship. I found many of the life stress milestones to be not only informative but related to my situation. You may have found that you relate to several of these examples. In the unlikely case where none of the descriptors or stress events pertained to you, realize that your best friend, family member, or the clerk at the grocery store may be suffering in silence. Now that we know what Empty Nest Syndrome is let's go one step further and review the five major symptoms parents may experience.

The Five Empty Nest Syndrome Symptoms

The symptoms of Empty Nest Syndrome are similar to the five stages of grief, not in their definition but in how they are negative feelings triggered by an event. In Elizabeth Kubler-Ross's book *On Death and Dying*, she proposed that individuals who experience the loss of someone close manage their grief by going through five stages:

- denial
- anger
- bargaining
- depression
- acceptance

Just as each stage has its own associated emotion, the same is true for a person with the Empty Nest Syndrome. There is the event of the child leaving the home. There are symptoms and emotions associated with each stage of that process. Parents can experience anxiety, loss, and sadness before, during, and after their child departs. Luckily, becoming an empty nester is not nearly as harsh and finite as death, but understanding and recognizing the symptoms of Empty Nest Syndrome, like understanding the five stages of grief, can help individuals and their support network identify, empathize, and potentially avoid negative feelings and outcomes.

Throughout my research, I came across many lists containing symptoms of Empty Nest Syndrome. Some articles listed the top three; Wikipedia stated six, while several blogs listed dozens. After compiling all the lists, I grouped the most common symptoms into five categories. The five most common Empty Nest Syndrome symptoms are:

1. **loss of identity**
2. **loss of control**
3. **emotional toll**
4. **relationship and individual stress**
5. **parenting anxiety**

I have summarized the collective critical points of each symptom in hopes that you will become both knowledgeable and able to identify these symptoms in yourself and others experiencing Empty Nest Syndrome.

Your Identity and Your Purpose

Before diving into symptom number one, loss of identity, I wanted to ground us on identity and purpose. I have always found it both fascinating and telling how people identify themselves. For example, when someone is allowed to introduce themselves to a group or another person for the first time, how do they usually sum up who they are? A child will introduce themselves by name, age, and grade. On the other hand, an adult starts with their name but then usually quotes their working title or work. Usually, the title is followed by a narrative of the company they work for, and then occasionally they might include an additional personal narrative. For example, "I'm Bob. I am an accountant at Google, and I live in Sunnyvale." This would be most people's default introduction, the standard work introduction. For others who choose not to lead with their career choice in their self-introduction, they may start with sexual preference, pronouns, relationship status, or with something as simple as where they grew up. There are seemingly endless ways to deliver an introductory self-summary, and if you reflect on your own experience, you will realize there are no right or wrong ways to do this.

My introduction started like the Bob example; I'd say my name, company, tenure, and job title for years. As dull as that seems, it was how I summed up who I was. Sometime in my thirties, I realized that my self-introduction seemed shallow and uninteresting. Who cares about where I work or what my title is? That introduction says very little about me and usually only leads to a conversation about work or my career choice. Is my work status the personal data that defines who I am? With this realization, I pivoted away from the career introduction and incorporated a more personal introduction, such as, "Hi, I am Anthony. I think I'm funny, and I have three children. In my spare time, I like to hike."

Introductions share what is essential to the individual, what we are proud of, and what interests us. This is our identity. Being a parent is a big part of our identity for many of us. Whether we acknowledge it or not, we have built self-worth through the experience of having, raising, and updating others on where we are in the growth cycle of our children. How many conversations have you had where your children were brought up? How often have you rattled off your child or children's ages, their grades, or what activities they do? My educated guess is you have done this an endless number of times.

This example feeds into the first Empty Nest Syndrome symptom, loss of identity. Being a parent and raising a child is a powerful thread of ourselves that we like to share with others. Your children's facts, data, names, ages, grades, and activities are an extension of who you are as a parent and person. Once I had children, they became my introduction. Essentially, becoming a father became my purpose. Your status, title, label, or whatever you associate yourself with should include being a parent, which is something you should be proud of and feel comfortable including in your introduction.

1. Loss of Identity

Loss is a common symptom of Empty Nest Syndrome, but the physical act of losing a child when they leave the home isn't the loss I'm referring to. Empty Nest Syndrome loss refers to a parent feeling a loss of identity as an active parent or primary caregiver. For a moment, contemplate the hours spent preparing meals, caring, chauffeuring, giving advice, and being an active and connected parent. From diapers to high school diplomas, rearing your child has likely been your most significant investment of time and energy since birth. It should come as no surprise that raising a child is a satisfying two-decade accomplishment and the cornerstone of one's identity.

> **From diapers to high school diplomas, rearing your child has likely been your most significant investment of time and energy since their birth.**

When a child leaves the home, a parent is still a parent, but the totality of the daily care, feeding, support, and counseling ends. Realizing that one's life as an active, involved, day-to-day parent is ending can be a lot to process. Understandably, this realization often comes with a sense of loss. Amy Morin, in the article "The Best Empty Nest Advice for Parents Whose Kids Are Leaving the Coop," states, "Not only will they [a parent] experience less contact and interaction with their children, but they may also experience an identity crisis of sorts." and "Parents who have identified as a 'soccer mom' or a 'stay-at-home dad' may suddenly wonder who they are or how they fit into the world. Some parents report feeling a lot of anxiety as they don't know what to do with their time. Others report feeling depressed as they experience a sense of loneliness."

A parent's common emotion is sadness that their child is less dependent on them. For single parents, this can be as simple as asking, "What is my role now? What is my new purpose?" Additionally, there may be regret or anxiety that they weren't closer or more available to their child in the past. This is often expressed as a feeling of a missed opportunity or questioning the relationship one has had with their child.

As the dynamics of dependence and independence change between a parent and child, parents can experience nervousness about the newly evolving relationship. Essentially, uncertainty sets in about where the parent stands in the relationship. For example, "What is my role as a parent moving forward? Am I a continued champion, an adult peer, or transitioning to a friend?" You will always be the parent, and they will always be your child; however, their maturity, distance, and independence will change your interactions and relationships.

Loss of identity is similar to loss of a job or primary responsibility. A parent experiencing this loss often gets stuck in a "what's my purpose now" mindset. They may think, "I have been parenting my child for eighteen years, now what?" Or question, "Is my work as a parent done?" Even if these questions don't specifically apply to you, all parents go through some measure of identity loss as their parenting responsibilities lessen when their child leaves the nest.

2. Loss of Control

The second primary Empty Nest Syndrome symptom is adjusting to the emotions and reality around the loss of control over one's child. Loss of control doesn't just pertain to the helicopter parent, characterized by excessive participation and hovering over a child, but all modern parents. Modern parenting today comes with the expectation that a parent has a dedicated, active role in raising their children. A parent is expected to marshal, support, counsel, and co-experience what their child is experiencing while growing up. A twenty-first-century parent lives in a highly connected world—one where they must actively set boundaries, curfews, and media stoppages. It is a world where they must monitor, supervise, and perhaps even stalk their children's whereabouts. Beyond keeping up with daily life, a parent is constantly setting standards and expectations about the outcomes they expect concerning almost everything their child does.

Does this sound like a lot of control? It is. Part of the definition of good parenting is being an active and involved parent. However, there is a downside. The ongoing control you may have fostered with your child has likely created a pattern. That pattern will change when it comes time for your child to leave home. You may find that you have little to no influence over your child's daily actions and choices. Along with the loss of influence, you won't be informed of your child's day as you have likely become accustomed to. When your child lives independently, this lack of information and contact can make any parent feel excluded. Even the strongest of parents can feel lonely, disconnected, and sad when entering this new era of being out of touch and perhaps feeling excluded. Spoiler alert: I felt this symptom most of all out of the five, but more about my situation later.

These feelings are natural. What was once part of your daily routine and your responsibility is no longer present. Your child's decision to attend class or not, study or work, date, eat, and hang out with friends is now beyond your sphere of influence. For a highly connected parent, these feelings and symptoms can be challenging to experience and adjust to. Much of your parenting life has been spent keeping your child safe and trying to control the world around them for the better. There is a loss of control. This loss can become stifling for a parent by losing and adjusting to the new dynamic of lack of control.

3. The Emotional Toll

When I was thirty-three years old, there was a one-month period when I started a new job, bought a house, and had my third child. Although each event was considered a positive milestone life event, each of these milestones came with stress and anxiety. The job I started was a new direction in my career in an unfamiliar industry. The house I bought was a fixer-upper that needed a lot of work, and my wife didn't want to move into it. When my third child was born, I had an active three-year-old, a two-year-old, and now a new baby, keeping our daily lives busy. It was a trying time to transition to a new job, move, and raise three children while keeping my sanity.

During this month of activity, I suddenly came down with shingles, a viral outbreak that can include a painful rash and blisters on my body. I had never experienced this, and I headed to the doctor immediately. I sat on the newly papered examination table, and the doctor asked, "So, what's going on in your life right now?" I replied with everything I just explained here. My doctor replied, "You have just experienced three major life events in one month, all of which induce stress. One of these events is manageable for most, but three are why you are sitting in my office." This moment was the first time I reflected on my stress and limits. Additionally, this event helped me realize that significant life events shouldn't be ignored or just experienced as they come. Still, it is healthy to anticipate, acknowledge, and seek help when you find yourself in a situation of stress or change.

Transitioning to becoming an empty nester may not be the same for each of us, but it is safe to say there will be some cause and effect that takes an emotional toll on you as a parent. For some parents, this may be a passing phase of emotions. For others, it can be a shingle-inducing reaction.

In more severe cases, it can be a lot worse, such as feelings of sadness and grief, which lead to depression. In an article titled "Factors Influencing the Quality of Life of empty nesters: Empirical Evidence from Southwest China," researchers studied 3,500 empty nesters in China as well as overseas. The study concluded that "children's departure from their home has visible impacts, including parents suffering from high levels of depression and loneliness." The research further states, "Without support from societal forces such as family, relatives, or even friends, the empty nesters suffer different risky circumstances such as unhappiness, losing sleep, and failing to overcome difficulties. These negative experiences can lead to depression, increased stress, anxiety, and other adverse symptoms, resulting in a reduced quality of life."

Even the parent excited to have their child leave may feel the emotional impact of change. A parent's love, commitment, and familiarity with their child as a consistent presence in their life can feel jeopardized or lost once a child leaves the home. It is common for parents to have thoughts such as, "I wonder what my child is doing? I miss them. Do they miss me?" These thoughts are not only typical but expected. As a parent, you have lived in a world where quickly checking in with your child was easy because they were within your physical radius. You could read their face, sense their emotions, and choose whether to react or not. Once out of the home, your immediate feedback loop is gone.

The impact of your child's absence can trigger feelings of sadness, worry, and stress. There is no standard emotion or universal way to react. Every author, article, and research paper presents an emotional basket of negative emotions parents may feel due to Empty Nest Syndrome. Healthline

Media's *PsychCentral* website cites Empty Nest Syndrome symptoms as being grief, emptiness, fear, worry, restlessness, loneliness, and irritability. Mind you, this is just one article. In some articles, the emotional toll is compared to the feelings of divorce or the loss of a loved one. Although most published content is slightly different, most boil down to emotional states such as sadness, depression, stress, and anxiety.

The emotional toll associated with Empty Nest Syndrome isn't just centered on the parent-child relationship. A child's departure can also bring about self-reflection, such as the realization that you are getting older, your life is changing, and you are moving into a new phase. With any significant change, it is common for an individual to reflect on their life. Since your child's daily care is over, your wants and needs may come to the forefront at this stage in your life. An empty nester can be happy and satisfied or potentially disillusioned or frustrated. Often, frustration is cited as one discovers they may not be financially, emotionally, or in a situation in life they expected to be at this stage. All emotions associated with Empty Nest Syndrome may not be welcome, but they are valid and concerning.

4. Relationship and Individual Stress

One of the symptoms of Empty Nest Syndrome is marital and individual stress. As any married couple can tell you, marital stress can occur for an endless number of reasons and be triggered by multiple internal and external forces, including work, finances, and family, to name a few. As a single empty nester, an ex or other family member could be involved. In that case, this situation might have heightened emotions as another parent or family member is dealing with the Empty Nest transition. In the case of a single or solo empty nest parent, stress during this time is commonplace as a two-decade dynamic is about to change.

Even in the most robust individual lives, much of a single parent's life may have included sacrificed personal pursuits for tending to life's responsibilities. This can also mean that an individual's well-being has been deprioritized. Over eighteen years of parenting, an individual can fall into routines where personal needs and aspirations are neglected, prioritizing external obligations over oneself. As the Empty Nest transition comes into view, such as children leaving home, the reality is that one needs to refocus one's personal growth and well-being. A single parent may find r-establishing a daily life just by focusing on themselves challenging. This transition can be stressful and lead to unplanned self-reflection and questioning.

Simple questions may arise as the "back to self-discovery" routine emerges, such as:

- What do I do now?
- What are my passions and interests?
- Do I still know myself?
- What do I want from life?
- Am I content with my own company?

The answers to these questions for the most well-balanced person on the planet can bring about stress and anxiety.

Additionally, some individuals may discover that their emotional experience of transitioning into a post-active parenting life varies significantly from their expectations. Many single empty nesters early on reportedly see this phase as an all-positive transition, while others dread embracing the new situation and routine. The difference or perception gap can be debilitating when expectations and emotions don't go as planned. What one thinks would be one way versus a new reality can bring stress and affect one's well-being. Thinking that a single parent can easily transition to an individual-focused routine after a significant period of life may be expecting too much. Many parents underestimate the impact of years of external focus and routine.

A single parent may find reestablishing a daily life just by focusing on themselves challenging.

5. Parenting Anxiety

Part of becoming an empty nester is letting go of the management, worry, and active aspects of managing your child. We know that letting go is part of a child growing up and maturing as an adult. You have experienced glimpses of this letting go as your children became potty trained, dressed themselves, fed themselves, and learned to drive. With each of these independent steps from your child, there was a shift in your role as a parent. You likely celebrated no more diapers, you were glad they started doing things independently, and you surely didn't miss chauffeuring them around and carpooling.

Throughout their growth process and as your child became more independent and self-reliant came an inevitability of new things they needed your help with. You shifted from taking care of simple basic needs to a more complex supportive role, such as giving relationship advice, guiding them through teen drama, and helping with stressful situations. The realization that they will be transitioning to complete self-reliance and that you will be physically separated from them defines this Empty Nest Syndrome symptom of parenting anxiety.

Anxiety and worry associated with the departure and separation of a child can come in many forms. Some parents are concerned about their children's ability to live independently and do the daily things they must do to care for themselves. Parents may worry about their child's ability to eat right, take medication, or maintain proper hygiene without their supervision. Beyond the worry of a child's self-care, many parents have safety concerns and worry about the social pressures their child will face living independently. A common concern of parents is wondering if their child is responsible enough not to put themselves in a situation where something negative could happen to them. Worrying about the responsible use of alcohol, avoiding risky behaviors, or just being aware of dangerous situations and surroundings can make the most confident parents feel anxiety. Although it is common for parents to have anxiety about what their child may or may not do, many parents have anxiety about whether they adequately prepared their child for a life outside of the home.

All of these examples, which are very common, can leave a parent or parents trapped in a cycle of concern and worry. Although discussed further in chapter 5, many parents battle their worries by hyper-communicating, which is defined as calling and texting their child excessively. Other parents attempt to continue helicopter parenting, such as stalking their child on social media, visiting their child too much, or trying to manage their child's life from afar. These behaviors underscore how worry and anxiety can not only affect a parent but also tamper a child's growth and independence away from home.

If you have ever been on a Facebook page for parents of attending college students, you can find numerous examples of parental fear, worry, and overreach. One of my favorite examples is when my wife stumbled upon a post in the parents' forum at our daughter's college. A parent posted,

"URGENT! MY SON NEEDS HELP." Upon seeing this, my wife became immediately concerned and clicked on the message. We later found out hundreds of other parents had done this as well. The message explained, "Help, there are no towel hangers in my son's dorm. Does anyone have a solution to this problem?" Mind you, this was from an adult parent. Urgent? Help? Really? This is an excellent example of parental overreach, and it underscores the parental anxiety and adjustment an empty nester can feel. My wife felt parenting anxiety when she read the subject line. For some parents, the self-doubt, anxiety, and worry they experience after their child leaves the home can be debilitating.

Symptoms Summary

Let's imagine a close friend sat you down and told you the following:

"You are going to adjust to a change in your personal and parental identity. You are going to let go of parental control. You are going to reevaluate your life. You are going to reflect on your parenting style. You are going to experience a variety of negative emotions and stress in tandem with your child."

The most put-together individual would indeed pause. This is probably one reason I'm not invited to parties anymore. Empty Nest Syndrome symptoms are experienced in degrees. Some can be minor and manageable, while others can be major and overwhelming. Becoming an empty nester brings change, and adjusting to change is never easy. In the worst-case scenarios, Empty Nest Syndrome can compound and spiral into depression. In the best-case scenario, understanding Empty Nest Syndrome leads to helping yourself and others with empathy and awareness.

There is no magic pill you can take to alleviate Empty Nest Syndrome; however, you can take multiple steps and actions to plan and prepare for this important stage in your life. The next chapter focuses on providing you with solutions to each of the syndromes we just explored.

CHAPTER 4 KEY POINTS

- Empty Nest Syndrome is when parents experience sadness and loss when the last child leaves home.

- Although some parents may be more predisposed to Empty Nest Syndrome, all parents are susceptible.

- A single parent or an individual such as a full-time parent tends to be more susceptible to Empty Nest Syndrome.

- Empty Nest Syndrome symptoms include loss of identity, loss of control, emotional toll, relationship and individual stress, and parenting anxiety.

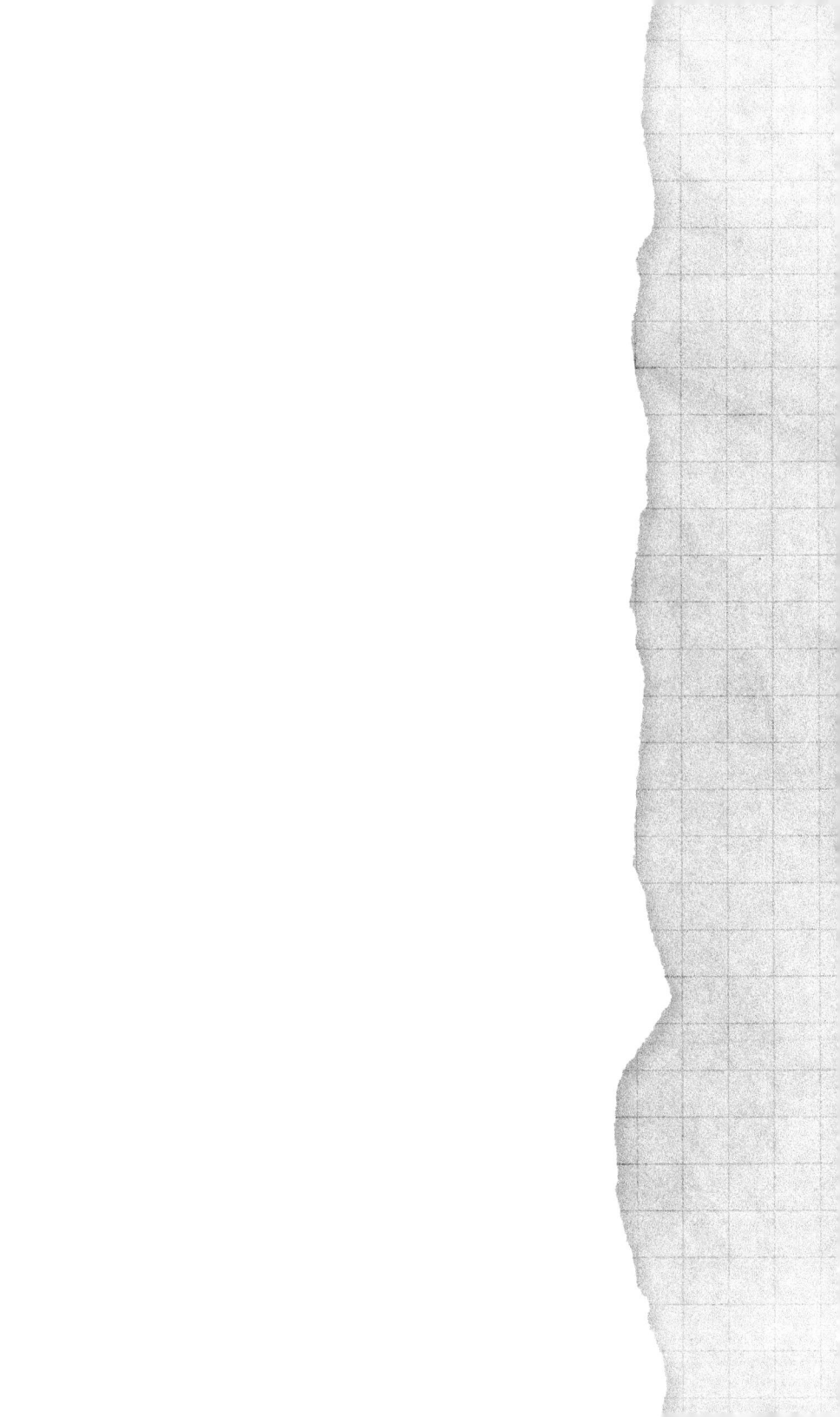

"It's not only children who grow. Parents do too. As much as we watch to see what our children do with their lives, they are watching us to see what we do with ours."

—JOYCE MAYNARD

CHAPTER FIVE

Symptoms to Solutions

WE CAN ALL agree that Empty Nest Syndrome is a natural phenomenon that can affect a parent in various ways. The purpose of the last chapter was to introduce Empty Nest Syndrome and categorize and explain the symptoms many parents experience. Now that you are more aware of what you and others in a similar situation may be facing, it's time to focus on solutions.

Although Empty Nest Syndrome can affect you, there are ways to cope, battle, and even thrive by taking action. As individuals, each of us will experience our own personalized Empty Nest journey. Just as one symptom or feeling you may

be experiencing may not be universal, neither is each solution. The overarching goal of this chapter is to arm you with options and choices to battle the most common symptoms and create solutions that resonate with you.

Many of the solutions here can be recommended across multiple symptoms. For example, having a support structure and someone to talk to would be a general recommendation to help someone struggling with each symptom. However, to avoid repetitiveness, I categorized each solution under the symptom most correlated with the research or most commonly associated with the symptom. Here is a list of the Empty Nest symptom and its corresponding solution.

SYMPTOM	SOLUTION
Loss of Purpose / Identity	Redefine Your Purpose
Loss of Control	Create Connection
The Emotional Toll	Seek Support
Relationship and Individual Stress	Embrace Your Individual Upside
Parenting Anxiety	Trust Your Work

Just as some of the symptoms of Empty Nest Syndrome are nuanced and complex, so are some solutions. I have tried to summarize each solution succinctly and thoroughly while incorporating a few personal experiences. Let's walk through each solution to arm ourselves with information, recommendations, and reference points.

1. Redefine Your Purpose

SYMPTOM	SOLUTION
Loss of Purpose / Identity	Redefine Your Purpose

It is not uncommon for a parent to find a new life's purpose when having a child. Most single parents dedicate themselves to raising a child and accept the excessive number of responsibilities placed on them as soon as the child is born. Spoken or unspoken, the new role of a parent transforms most people's lives. In the same regard, once a child leaves home and no longer needs to be actively raised, essentially becoming less dependent on their parent, the parent can feel their role has diminished, and their purpose is lost.

The first thing to do is recognize and accept that change is happening. Your child is leaving, and your role is changing. Congratulate yourself on the time and effort you spent raising your child over the last two decades. This is a time to celebrate a job well done and realize that this change can bring personal satisfaction and enjoyment.

One of the most significant changes you will experience when your child leaves home is more free personal time. You will have fewer interruptions, a quieter home, one less person to manage, and fewer distractions. On the surface, this list can seem sad, but your child's absence creates an opportunity for you to focus on yourself and what you deem necessary. You are now in an enviable position to explore your ambitions, new opportunities, hobbies, and interests that you may have been putting on the backburner since actively parenting. You have a purpose as an empty nester beyond active parenting. That purpose is focusing on you.

Redefine Your Identity

Being a parent is an identity for life. Just because your child is leaving the nest doesn't mean you relinquish your parental title the next day. Yes, if you have been introducing yourself as a stay-at-home dad or mom, perhaps a title change is in order, but again, you are still a parent. You are merely no longer actively raising a child.

Your identity comprises all the distinguishing character or personality traits you possess. Remember, before you had children, you were still you. Your children may define you as a parent, but they don't define who you are. It's okay if raising your children has been your greatest accomplishment. That is something all parents should be proud of. After all, your children are your legacy. But if you are struggling to lose your title or label, you can quickly reinvent a new label. You can easily pivot from being "Tina's mom" or a "stay-at-home mom" to something like, "I am a mother of three who likes to…" Whatever you decide to fill in that blank is how you redefine yourself.

> **Your children may define you as a parent, but they don't define who you are.**

Beyond the surface-level title or label change, the loss of identity as an Empty Nest Syndrome symptom tends to be more internally focused. The world will see you as how you present yourself to it (e.g., Irish-Italian, mother of five, attorney at law). When you become an empty nester, the identity struggle is more about how you define and see yourself.

Your identity is all about self-realization. You have never been only one thing. There are a multitude of experiences, traits, skills, and mysteries that make up the foundation of who you are.

Redefining your identity is not easy. Hopefully, with some self-realization and focusing on your positive traits, you can be what you decide to be in your next chapter in life. You have always been more than a parent.

2. From Control to Connection

SYMPTOM	SOLUTION
Loss of Control	Create Connection

There is no way to deny it. You cannot raise a child without some semblance of control. Control comes in many forms for a parent, from guidance to rules, expectations to discipline, and freedom to restriction. As you have raised and guided your child throughout their lives, you have exerted control for their safety, well-being, growth, and development. Once your child leaves home, it is often that first leap of their self-independence and responsibility that can leave you feeling a loss of control. Health eUniversity in Canada, a Cardiovascular Prevention and Rehabilitation Program, sums up one's sense of control well. They state, "Your sense of control is how much control you feel over your life. Having the right amount of control is what helps keep you balanced. Feeling that you have no control can lead to anxiety or depression."

One of the first things you should realize in order to combat a loss of control is that feeling uneasy about your child leaving the home is normal. Many parents struggle with relinquishing control over their children as they transition independently. Common anxiety and concerns include worrying about how they are adjusting to a new location, potentially being introduced to risky behavior (college partying), or just an uneasiness that they might be naïve or unaware of everyday dangers around them. Although these concerns can be discussed with your child, dwelling on them after their departure is counterproductive. There are four things you can do to lessen the impact of loss of control you have on your child. Here is a brief overview of each connection solution:

1. **Plan for Departure**
2. **Discuss Concerns (Theirs, Then Yours)**
3. **Decide Communication Expectations**
4. **Be Their Rock**

1. Plan for Departure

One of the first things you can do, ideally before your child leaves the nest, is come to terms with the timing of their departure. Creating a mental or physical pre-launch timeline will allow you to plan for their departure and consider, discuss, and potentially resolve any issues or topics that may worry you or your child. In the best-case scenario, this time will allow you to reflect and adjust to your future state and prepare your child for independent living. Sitting down with your child the night before they leave home is not an excellent way to cover the litany of things you may wish to discuss with them (budgets, behavior, communication, academic expectations, etc.). If you have a timeline, use it to your advantage and discuss different topics over this pre-launch period. This will ensure you both have time to process any requests from each other and understand expectations.

2. Discuss Concerns (Theirs, Then Yours)

As a parent, having a list of concerns surrounding your child's upcoming life outside the home is normal. It would be best to discuss your concerns with your child; however, since there are two parties in this example, you and your child, it is a good idea to start these conversations not with your concerns but by exploring any worries or fears they have. For example, before my third daughter left for college, she was very concerned about trends and activities related to physical assault against women at college. I also had these same concerns, but the fact that she brought it up meant that I could follow her lead instead of initiating the topic. This is also a great example of feeling a loss of control. Her safety is obviously one of my top concerns, yet I cannot control any future situations or be there to protect her. During this conversation, I listened to her concerns and fears and probed her understanding of how she would avoid situations where an assault may happen. For example, I counseled her to never go to a party, bar, or gathering alone. Always use a buddy system, always go out with a roommate, and agree that you will attend together and, most importantly, leave together at the end of the night.

Throughout our conversation, I realized this was something she fully understood and was already planning on doing, which alleviated some of my anxiety. There were additional topics I brought up that she knew, but I just needed to say them to get confirmation she understood. For example, we talked about not leaving a drink unattended and not drinking things just given to you. We discussed her using campus police and campus shuttles and her being fully informed of the safety measures all colleges market to parents and students during their college tours. I realized safety was a significant control issue, which I needed to acknowledge and relinquish.

This was just a snippet of the broader conversation we had about safety. Frankly, there is an endless list of common-sense things you will have to trust your child has picked up on with any given topic. We didn't talk about locking doors, carrying pepper spray, or keeping backpacks, purses, and electronics hidden from view in a locked car. Again, a list of pre-departure topics can be endless and will be different for every child based on their maturity, personality, and upbringing. Topics covered in totality for my three children included safety, self-care, academic expectations, lifestyle, finances, and support systems. As each child was different, some topics didn't need to be covered, while others were on top of the list. One child needed to learn how to do laundry while another already cooked, cleaned, and knew all the basics.

Probe your child to hear their concerns, allowing you to express your own. If you can have these conversations in a cooperative brainstorming way rather than a dictatorial list of problems you have for them, your discussion will be richer, and your points will be more likely to stick. If that approach doesn't work, review your list so nothing is left unsaid.

After each conversation, you must remind yourself they have accepted the responsibility; therefore, it is no longer your responsibility. Let go of the control. The occasional subtle reminder is okay, but you had the safety talk at the end of the day. It's now their job to remain safe.

3. Decide Communication Expectations

In almost all of my research, when the topic of children leaving home is discussed, communication is the number-one suggestion a parent should discuss with their child. It is common for parents to know what type and frequency of communication they want with their child, just as their child may have their thoughts on this topic. Ideally, parent and child are in the same ballpark. Some children want to check in daily, while others are good with a text once a month. Many parents set up a recurring check-in time, like Sunday evenings. Others let communication happen naturally. Your child's departure is about fostering their development and independence, so I recommend letting them drive communication frequency.

My communication research repeatedly mentioned two traps for parents and children to avoid: hyper-connecting and taking things personally. Modern parents have become accustomed to having their children available at their conversational whim for the last eighteen years. A hyper-connecting parent does not need an hourly or daily report of their child's day. Initially, many parents struggle with this aspect of their child's departure. Still, they soon discover that stepping back and giving a child space to reach out on their terms fosters independence and growth and can make for a richer discussion when contact is initiated.

Hyper-connecting can also occur in reverse. Your child may be initiating and consistently coming to you with issues or problems or feel they need to give you a complete rundown of their life. Every parent-child relationship is different; some children greatly rely on their parents. Work within your comfort zone, but you must help your child grow and develop independently. This may mean you must pivot from being the constant go-to problem solver to the listener. You will always help your child and support them, but it's also essential to encourage them to problem-solve themselves. This can be especially difficult for the habitual problem-solving parent (guilty as charged) whose child has always relied on them. Awareness of this communication trap should help most parents reflect and find a balance.

The final communication trap repeatedly mentioned is when parents take a lack of communication from their child personally. Many parents equate a child not reaching out, missing a scheduled call, or not texting back immediately as a demonstration of the child being disinterested or uncaring. If we all honestly reflect on our late teens and early twenties, it's safe to assume that our parents' well-being was not at the top of our social and daily routine. When children depart the home, they have a lot of adjustments and discoveries to do with their newfound independence. They may be busy working, taking classes, exploring friendships, or having some downtime in their own space. A college student's day can be endlessly filled with people, things to do, and places to explore.

In most cases, there is no malicious intent in forgetting to call one's parent or not connecting as often as a parent may like. Every author on this subject recommended that parents should not make their children feel guilty or take it personally if there is a lack of communication. Getting upset or lecturing your child about missed calls or making them feel bad about their lack of communication will only sour the openness and connection you wish to foster. The more you embrace their independence and encourage personal growth, the better.

4. Be Their Rock

This should go without saying, but before your child leaves your home, let them know you are in their corner, you support them, and you believe in them. Although this can be a bit cliché, it is vital that they truly understand that you are a haven for them throughout their lives.

We know that most teens at eighteen think they know more than they do. They have also likely developed a good sense of stubbornness and pride. Don't let these traits hinder you from being their rock. The last thing you want your child to feel is ashamed, embarrassed, or unsure that they can reach out to you when needed. Let them know they have a home to return to, and if they find themselves in a sticky situation, they can rely on you for help. You can share with them that you understand that their newfound independence will include challenges and struggles. All the prior advice centers on embracing your child's independence and growth and relinquishing control. You are encouraging independence with the assurance of your love and support. Letting your child know you are in their corner and will be there for them is the greatest thing you can do for them.

Beyond communicating to your child that you are their number-one support system, this is an opportunity for you to discuss your emotions with your child before they leave. If you are feeling sad, share your thoughts and feelings with them in a guilt-free manner. If you can make the conversation positive, that would be great. If the discussion is centered around negative emotions, share those emotions with a balance of the positive aspects of the situation. For example, "Although I will miss you greatly, I am excited about your next chapter at college." One suggestion is not just to tell them that you'll miss them but to tell them what you'll miss about them, turning the negative into a compliment. Another suggestion is to make them aware that this is not only an exciting time of adjustment for them but also an adjustment for you. Discussing concerns, emotions, and feelings about your child's departure with them is okay. Still, it is essential to balance that in sharing their excitement, encouraging their growth, and being optimistic about their future as they head out.

One suggestion is not just to tell them
that you'll miss them but to tell them
what you'll miss about them, turning
the negative into a compliment.

3. Seek Support

SYMPTOM	SOLUTION
The Emotional Toll	Seek Support

There is no one way to parent, celebrate, or grieve. We are all different and handle situations differently. The same is true for the emotions and support you may need when your child leaves the nest. For some parents, the transition is easy. You may experience moments of sadness or briefly miss your child. For others, separation, anxiety, and sadness can be debilitating. Some people may need very little emotional support while others may need a lot. You can boldly assume that you or your best friend will transition to an Empty Nest in stride, but your assumption may be completely wrong.

Many of us, even the most self-aware and confident, may not feel the impact of our Empty Nest transition until it happens. Recognizing that there may be an emotional toll on you and others is the first step in being able to seek support or be support for others. There are four major support solutions I uncovered in my research. They are:

1. **Friends and Family**
2. **Support Forums**
3. **Do-It-Yourself Approach**
4. **Professional Help**

I will briefly touch on each support solution.

1. Friends and Family

Talking about becoming an empty nester and its associated emotions is one way to garner support. By opening up to a family member or friends, you share your feelings and potentially help others feel they are not alone. This book was written on this premise. You, your sibling, your best friend, or the person you just met at a cocktail party may be experiencing some emotional burden with their Empty Nest transition. Others may have experienced it, are going through it with you, or will experience it in the future. By diving into this topic and bringing it into a conversation, you have now equipped yourself with the knowledge to identify symptoms, understand struggles, and hopefully share these solutions and your successes with others.

Before jumping in and helping others, let's return to helping you deal with the emotions of becoming an empty nester. The first key to success is to not go through this process alone. This is an ideal time to leverage your support network and share how you are feeling and what you are experiencing.

If you were to open up to a friend and say, "James is leaving for college next month, and I will miss him," you will probably receive a kind, placated reply in return. To get the next level of support, you will want to be more vulnerable and bring relevancy and seriousness to the conversation. You can use the symptom or solution headings in the last two chapters as conversation starters. It can be as simple as, "With James leaving for college next month, I feel anxious about my role and purpose moving forward. I have dedicated myself as a full-time parent for so long, and now I feel a bit lost." The keywords here are anxious, role, purpose, and feeling lost. There are a multitude of feelings and emotions you can tie into a conversation with a friend. Still, by pairing what you are feeling with some of the labels outlined in the last chapter, you will likely have a much more relevant and rewarding conversation.

Other avenues for support would be to contact friends and family who have gone through this transition in the past and seek their advice and counsel on how they dealt with it. Alternatively, you can contact parents you know or those in your wider circle of friends who are experiencing this phenomenon with you.

Wrapping up this section, you didn't raise your child alone, and you are not alone when going through this transition. Talk to others in your support network and share how you feel. It is okay to reach out for support, and you will find others will feel better by helping you. Also, realize that many others in the same situation may face similar challenges. Preferably, you can both gain support and be supportive of others.

2. Support Forums

If you find yourself in a situation where you may not have a support system around you or your support system isn't sympathetic, you still have many options to find the support you need. Almost every college and military branch has parent-focused support forums on social media. Facebook can be a primary source. Most colleges and universities have two support forum groups. The first is a parent-led forum where you give or seek advice from other parents. Usually these forums are organized by graduating year. This is an excellent resource for a parent, with the added benefit that all group members are first-year students and that most topics, suggestions, and questions are relevant to all members. "URGENT, you can find a towel rack."

The second type of college and university forum is a school-sponsored parent and family forum. This is usually a discussion group of information that the school maintains. My youngest daughter's university parent and family forum states, "We provide an extension of our services to all parents and families of our student body." Like any public forum, these groups cover various topics and discussions from contributing parents, counselors, and faculty.

The overarching advantage of these parent and school-run groups is that they keep you connected to what is happening at the school and what other parents are experiencing. This underscores that you are not alone. My experience when joining these groups, as I did with my three children's schools, was that I found many other parents from all walks of life experiencing the same phenomenon of a child leaving home. Many of these forums and popular parent forums on Facebook are informative, active, and generally very supportive of questions and advice.

3. Do-It-Yourself Approach

There is no shame in discussing your feelings, having a conversation, or needing support from others as you transition to an Empty Nest. Beyond the recommendation of reaching out to others, a subset of people may prefer to go through this process alone. My recommendation for individuals in the do-it-yourself camp would be to focus on themselves first. Acknowledge how you are feeling and give yourself time to process any feelings and adjust to the change in your life.

One supportive activity you can engage in beyond reading this book during this time is journaling your thoughts and feelings. The act of just writing down how you are feeling often immediately alleviates some anxiety and can be very therapeutic. Another suggestion is to take up meditation. You can download many available applications and use their guided meditation to help clear your thoughts while allowing yourself some time to relax. Overall, this is a joyous time in your child's life and your own. Keeping this realization in front of your mind is an excellent focal point when feeling down.

4. Professional Help

If leveraging others or going through this journey alone fails to help you, or if you find yourself overwhelmed or needing more focused support, professional counseling is a healthy option.

While sadness, loneliness, and anxiety can be associated with Empty Nest transitions, these emotions can spiral into a more severe diagnosis of depression and isolation. Although this is reported as a rare occurrence, professional counseling is an excellent alternative if an individual needs help beyond what they feel their support groups are providing.

The American Counseling Society states, "Professional counselors help clients identify goals and potential solutions to problems which cause emotional turmoil; seek to improve communication and coping skills; strengthen self-esteem; and promote behavior change and optimal mental health." If available, check with your employer's benefits department to see if counseling is included in your benefits package. You may find that you have some assistance available at a low or no cost. If these benefits aren't available, you can pursue online resources to access professional help.

4. Individual Upside

SYMPTOM	SOLUTION
Relationship and Individual Stress	Embrace Your Individual Upside

Having your child leave the home while adjusting to a new life post-children can be stressful. However, becoming an empty nester doesn't mean you are on a negative track. You can do many things to turn your situation into a positive transition rather than letting stress dominate your headspace.

My first recommendation is to eliminate the element of surprise. Do not wait until the dorm room college drop-off day to consider your new life as an empty nester. Take the time, pre-drop off, to explore the emotions you believe you will feel and create long-term goals. We will explore this more in chapter 16, "Your Plan for Your Child." The more you mentally prepare for your Empty Nest transition before it happens, the better. Of course, you should explore the thoughts and feelings you are experiencing and expect to encounter. But just thinking about your Empty Nest transition might lead to stress, whereas making decisions and plans for your future before your child leaves can build excitement and anticipation. In the ideal scenario, you are mentally preparing for the future and going through this experience with a broad understanding of the transition from individual emotions to future actions. As such, this can be a time for excitement and exploration of your future self.

Do not wait until the dorm room college drop-off day to consider your new life as an empty nester.

The second recommendation is to focus on the potential positives. You can use your upcoming Empty Nest status to explore everything you might want in the future, from changing your daily routine to the possibility of having the house and your lives to yourself once again. Beyond the immediate changes, look further ahead and use this time to think through what plans you can create. Can you now leverage this extra time to pursue something you want? Open-ended questions include, "What should I do with my extra time? What have I always wanted to do, or where have I wanted to go?" The answers to these questions may now be possible with your transition to an empty nester.

This is a time to accentuate the positive things you have been thinking about with your new Empty Nest status. For example:

- You have an opportunity to start up a new relationship/date.
- You can spend more time focusing on your physical and mental health.

- You can now connect with friends or family members you haven't had time to see.
- You have more time for interests, hobbies, or shared experiences.
- You may now be in a position to pursue things you have wanted to do that time constraints and parenting obligations previously prevented.

In some ways, the world is now your oyster, as time allows you to focus on yourself. Go out with friends, join a club or sports team, find a buddy, and attend sporting events or concerts you didn't have time for in the past. Take that hot bath, listen to your music whenever you want, or binge-watch something distraction-free. Thinking through, planning, or getting some of these ideas can introduce excitement and fun into your new Empty Nest life. More of this will come when we build your Empty Nest Blueprint in chapter 13.

The overarching solution to mitigating the symptoms of stress throughout your empty nester transition is to acknowledge your situation and focus on the endless positive things you can explore in your future. Just thinking about planning for your Empty Nest future will reduce the anxiety and surprise and lessen the stress during this change. In the following chapters, we will dive deeper into the Empty Nest relationships, detailing pitfalls and possibilities and expanding on proactive ways you can thrive as an empty nester.

5. Trust Your Work

SYMPTOM	SOLUTION
Parenting Anxiety	Trust Your Work

It is impossible to raise, nurture, and guide a child into early adulthood and not have moments of parental anxiety. There are countless examples of us as parents feeling this anxiety: dropping off our children on their first day of school, letting them spend the night at a friend's house for the first time, or watching them take the car keys and drive independently. You have spent your entire life trying to mitigate issues, avoid problems, and keep them safe. Now, they are embarking on a new life of their own, away from the security of your presence and active involvement. This situation can be anxiety-inducing for the best parents.

Throughout your child's lifetime, you have instilled your core values, which they have adopted as their own. You have taught them endless lessons on right and wrong and dealing with difficult situations. You have set expectations, goals, and standards that your child has achieved. Yes, there have likely been some roadblocks and failures along the way, but even these failed situations have become lessons for them. You have already set into motion the tools they need to address any problem they may find themselves in. They know they can come to you for help if they can't figure it out.

The fact that your child is now a young adult and ready to move out on their own proves you have done an excellent job getting them to this point. Be confident that you have laid a foundation for their continued independence. This is a time for self-congratulations. Once your child leaves, their personal growth will accelerate. Like every other child that has left the nest, they will survive. Trust me, your child will not starve. They will clean their clothes. They will brush their teeth. They will show up to classes and work. Perhaps some of these things won't be perfect or may happen over time, but your child will learn from their mistakes and become more self-reliant, just as you did. In most cases, you can expect your child to continue to live and thrive in a new environment.

We have focused thus far on the anxiety parents feel when their child leaves the nest; however, what we haven't focused on is you. Another recommendation to avoid or cope with parental anxiety is to step back from a child-focused framework and focus on yourself. Your child is embarking on a new life with new challenges in a new environment, so this is an opportunity for you to do the same. This is a time for you to focus on yourself. As stated earlier, you can manage your stress by relaxing, meditating, connecting with friends, exercising, pursuing your interests, and listening to music. Keeping yourself active will benefit you and your surrounding relationships and give you things to discuss with your child, underscoring that you are doing fine in their absence. By focusing on yourself and your new situation positively, you will find that dwelling on the what-if scenarios wastes your time.

Solutions Summary

Over the last two chapters, we have explored Empty Nest Syndrome. We have learned what Empty Nest Syndrome is and its common symptoms. We have explored recommended solutions to lessen, if not eliminate, potential adverse outcomes.

SYMPTOM	SOLUTION
Loss of Purpose / Identity	Redefine Your Purpose
Loss of Control	Create Connection
The Emotional Toll	Seek Support
Relationship and Individual Stress	Embrace Your Individual Upside
Parenting Anxiety	Trust Your Work

Although we have just reviewed Empty Nest Syndrome and solutions, we haven't explored the dynamics of becoming an empty nester or how our past influences have brought us to where we are today.

In the next chapter, we will go back to where it all started, with your parents. We will look at their influence and additional factors that gave you a foundational perspective on your parenting style and perhaps an Empty Nest role model.

CHAPTER 5 KEY POINTS

🖋 You can combat the five Empty Nest Syndrome symptoms with solutions

🖋 Each Empty Nest Syndrome solution can be helped by leveraging a support structure,

🖋 All solutions involve self-introspection, while some focus on yourself and your child.

🖋 Empty Nest Syndrome solutions include Redefine Your Purpose, Connection, Seeking Support, Individual Upside, and Trust Your Work.

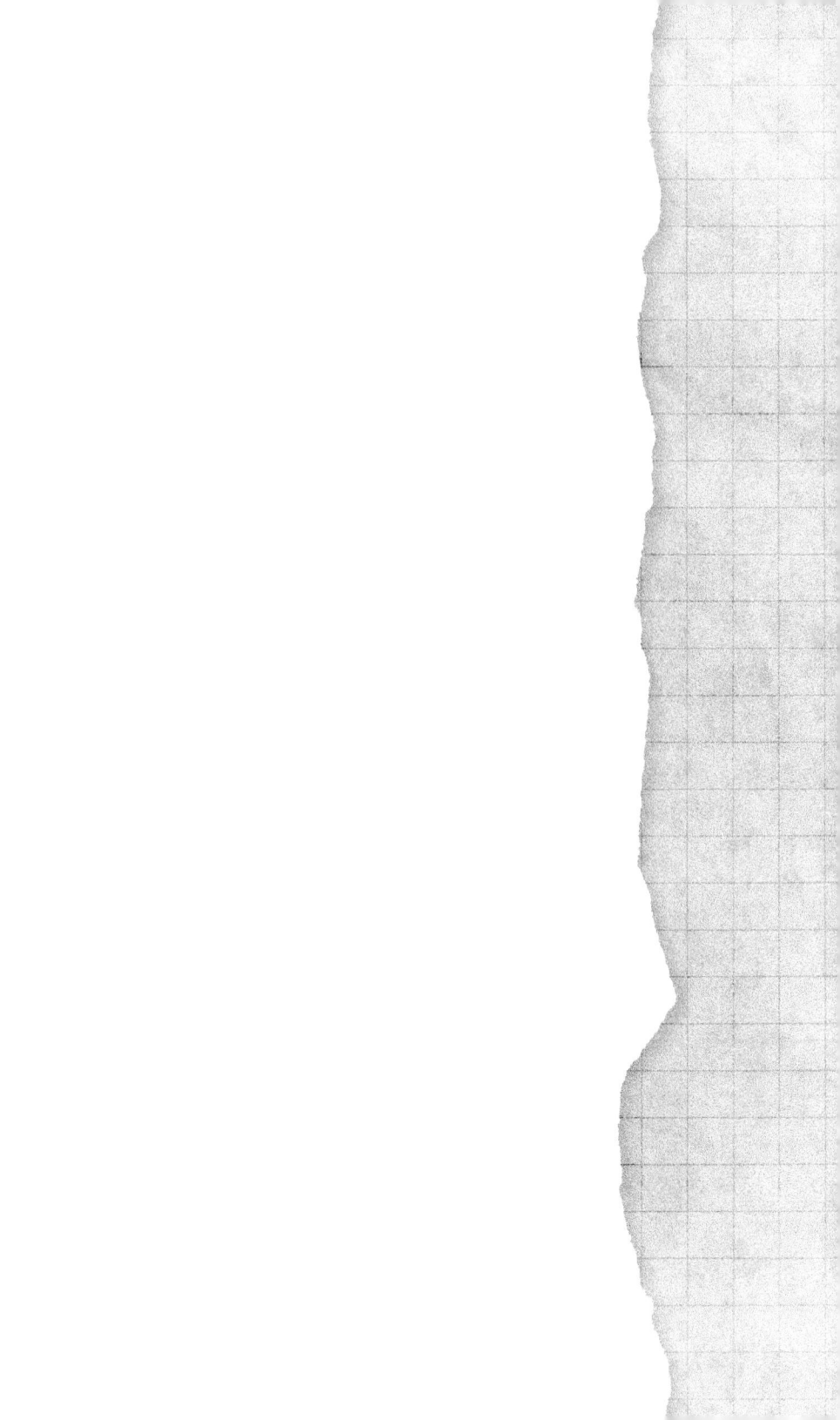

"I would say to any single parent currently feeling the weight of stereotype or stigmatization that I am prouder of my years as a single mother than of any other part of my life."

— J.K. ROWLING

CHAPTER SIX

Parenting DNA

Reflection

BECOMING AN EMPTY nester is an inflection point in your life. It is a time of endings, a time for continuation, and a time for new beginnings. Yes, the physical move of your child from your home is the epicenter of what is happening; however, the backdrop of your perspective is painted by your experience and relationships. Your relationship with your child, your friends, and yourself will inevitably come to the

surface as you experience an Empty Nest through the eyes of a parent. This time is an opportunity to understand and explore your relationships and feelings and an ideal time to decide what you want in each relationship moving forward. Like any critical inflection point, you can gain key insights and be better prepared to plan your future by examining and understanding your past.

This chapter is focused on your parenting DNA. You are a unique and complex person. Combining all your experiences and influences as a parent and individual has made you who you are today. This chapter aims to make you aware of your past experiences and influences to understand how and why you became who you are as a parent.

Throughout this chapter, I will share my story with prompts intended for you to reflect on your past. Essentially, you will be doing your self-discovery in parallel with me. Ideally, by reflecting on how we became the parents we are today, we will understand our internal relationship drivers and gain insights into why we act and feel the way we do. Furthermore, once armed with this information, you should be better equipped to make any decisions or changes as your Empty Nest future approaches.

Parenting DNA

There is a debate about whether parenting is instinctual or learned. Most agree that core survival instincts include caring, protecting, and loving a child. All mammals, to some degree, care for their young instinctively. These instincts are not necessarily learned but happen due to the emotional bond between parent and child. That said, it is scientifically accepted that, beyond the basic survival instincts of a parent, parenting skills are acquired.

Let's start with you. How did you acquire your parenting skills? Did you read a book, have a good teacher, or did it all come naturally? You likely learned your parenting skill set from a variety of sources, such as observing your parents' actions, your own experience, trial and error of your parenting practices, observing others, and being aware of what your particular child needs. There is a lot in that answer to unpack. Let's find answers to where our journeys started by examining our parenting DNA.

Our first experience with parenting came to us through observation. As children, we didn't actively take notes or train to be parents, but much of what we saw and experienced became a standard for our parenting style. Your parents acted in a specific way when you were growing up, which is what you learned. Interestingly, you only knew what you observed, interpreted, or were told. Motivational speaker Anthony Robbins has a good quote: "Your experience of life is not life; it's the few things your brain can focus on at one time." Observation and interpretation are funny in that you, your parents, and your siblings could experience the same event and come away from that event with a completely different perspective.

For example, let's say you had an older brother who came home one night after curfew, and you overheard your parents talking with him in the family room. Your parents could have been worried sick and extremely upset yet seemed calm. Your brother could have been terrified but pretended to be brave. In this scenario, you observed and interpreted the encounter as a peaceful and easy discussion, but you could have been entirely wrong.

The good news is that the totality of your childhood experience is not a one-time event memory. You grew up observing your parents firsthand. Their values, beliefs, and mannerisms were displayed for you to adhere to, adopt, or consider. It is reasonable to assume that your parents' techniques, quirks, personality traits, and rules were repeated enough throughout your childhood that you could understand and anticipate your parents' parenting style. Since all of us experienced a unique upbringing based on our parents' varied styles, I believe it would be helpful to ground ourselves using standard parenting style definitions.

Parenting Styles

Developmental psychologist Diana Baumrind and researchers Eleanor Maccoby and John Martin at Stanford University defined four parenting styles: permissive, authoritative, neglectful, and authoritarian. I've summarized each of the four styles here so we can quickly review and reference them.

The goal is for you to identify your parents' parenting style and understand your own. Trust me, this will be fun.

The Permissive Parent

Simply put, a permissive parent tends to take on a friendship role, avoids conflict, and gives in to their child's wants and demands when faced with a challenge. That screaming child in line in the grocery store who wants the candy bar will get the candy bar under the permissive parenting style. In this parenting dynamic, rules and expectations are either not set or rarely enforced. The permissive parent communicates openly with their child, allowing them to decide things for themselves. The parents' main goal is to make their children happy, sometimes at their own expense.

The Authoritative Parent

Don't confuse authoritative with authoritarian. An authoritative parenting style is one in which a parent is supportive, nurturing, and often on the same wavelength as their children's needs. They set clear rules and listen to and consider their children's thoughts, feelings, and opinions. This type of parent is generally both flexible and understanding. In turn, children raised with an authoritative parenting style tend to be self-disciplined and think for themselves.

The Neglectful Parent

This parenting style is best described as laissez-faire, an attitude of letting things take their course without interfering. A neglectful parent is uninvolved, often has limited engagement, and establishes few rules and expectations. On a developmental level, a neglectful parent would be indifferent to their child's emotional or behavioral needs, and they let their child figure it out on their own. Parents using this style come across as cold or uncaring, but they often struggle with their feelings, relationships, and issues, which causes them to disengage from their children.

The Authoritarian Parent

This parenting style is commonly defined as strict parenting. Authoritarian parents use discipline and tough love to bend their children's will. When it comes to rules and expectations, there is a one-way relationship from parent to child. In the end, an authoritarian parenting style is one where parents want to fully control their child and the situation without wanting or soliciting any input or feedback from their child. This child does not get the candy bar in the grocery line.

Applying the Four Styles

I have several quick notes from these examples before you assign your parents and your style. A parent using these styles may love, care for, and want what's best for their child. They may firmly believe their chosen style is the best for their situation. Although some parenting styles may seem harsh, strong influences such as religious and cultural norms may shape the actions of a parent. There is no judgment in the style a parent may have used, especially if they just adopted the style they were exposed to in their youth by their parents.

> **Although some parenting styles may seem harsh, strong influences such as religious and cultural norms may shape the actions of a parent.**

Furthermore, in many situations, one parent may have adopted one style whereas the other did something completely different. Did you ever ask one parent to go somewhere or do something only to hear no? And after not liking that answer, did you ask the other parent who said yes? Of course you did. This typical example underscores parenting differences. The four parenting styles would be extreme if adhered to by any parent 100 percent of the time. What may be more common is having a dominant style but situationally moving between styles.

Now that all the disclaimers are out, did you find your father's and mother's dominant styles? How about your style? Are you authoritarian or permissive? Are you more authoritative or neglectful? Like it or not, good or bad, much of our parenting style and principles come from what our parents did. If you had great parents, you likely adopted the same belief system, values, and traditions you experienced growing up. Hopefully, all the good of what you viewed and experienced formed your parenting style foundation.

In contrast, let's say you found yourself on the other end of the spectrum. You had less-than-stellar parents or perhaps only one present parent. The learned approach still holds. Chances are, what you experienced and learned has consciously or subconsciously modeled your parenting behavior. This doesn't mean if you had less-than-stellar parents that you became a less-than-stellar parent yourself. This only means you had to consciously change learned behaviors and adopt new ones instead of defaulting to your parent(s)' style. For many in this situation, adopting a situational model to "not do what my parents did" can be equally impactful and beneficial as just repeating what you experienced. A great example of this is a parent who grew up with an absent father or mother. Many parents in this situation consciously decide to be the opposite, a present and active parent, thus breaking any generational cycle.

Most of us have adopted the good parenting concepts we received from our parents and modeled those to our children. We also likely held onto the strong values, beliefs, and traditions we were comfortable with. We took the good we liked and perhaps even improved upon what we knew and experienced. At the same time, we learned from the bad experiences we had as a child and tried not to repeat them ourselves in our parenting role. For example, my father never changed a diaper. I longed to attend summer camp, but my parents couldn't afford it. My parents didn't pay for cars, gas, insurance, college, or fancy clothes. In contrast, I changed diapers. Our children went to summer camps. And I worked hard to provide my children with many of the things my parents didn't or couldn't afford. Social changes and wanting things for my children that I didn't have were prominent parental drivers for me.

As you reflect on your parent style and generational parenting modifications, it's easy to compare and contrast the differences. You may undervalue your parents' impact and point out their mistakes. You may also appreciate the positive contributions they made as parental role models. If parenting is generational, then your parents' actions were likely driven by their parents. They did what they experienced growing up and what was also socially expected of them then.

My Parents

I grew up with an authoritarian father (the strict one). We had stringent rules in our household, and when things went wrong, we were spanked and punished. We lived with father-based parental fear. There are endless examples of what this was like, but a good example is when my father drove into the driveway every day after work. No matter what my three siblings or I were doing, we would stop immediately and run into our bedrooms. Our father loved us, and we loved him, but since he was the definition of the authoritarian parent, my siblings and I grew up with some fear of our father. There were moments when he situationally adopted the three other parenting styles, but his dominant style was authoritarian.

Trying to categorize my mother's style is a bit more complicated. Many of her actions counterbalanced my father's. At times, she was permissive, letting us get our way. Other times, she let my father's authoritarian style dominate uncontested. Her dominant style was authoritative, trying to be good counsel and understand our needs.

There are thousands of more qualified and in-depth books on parenting, so I will keep this example short. Although I didn't necessarily have the perfect household as a child, there are reasons why my father and mother were the way they were. In the simplest of terms, they adopted their parents' styles. My father's mother died when he was ten years old. At the same time, his father was a strict "use the belt" disciplinarian.

I could stop the example here and justify his parental style in that he had little nurturing with the loss of his mother while being raised by a very strict father. His parenting style was 100 percent experienced and learned.

Further, my father enlisted in the military reserves right out of college and became a very buttoned-up, disciplined spouse and father. He started teaching high school when he was just a few years older than the seniors sitting in his classroom. To make matters worse, the high school students at this particular time, the late '60s and early '70s, had changed from his upbringing and generation a few years prior. Instead of students being obedient rule followers and respecting the authority of teachers and adults in the 1950s, my father's classroom challenged authority and social norms with "free love" and the boundary-pushing hippie movement.

Rather than relating to his students, they generationally scared my father. By the late '60s, my father had four young children, and he didn't much like what the younger hippie generation in his classroom was doing. Looking back, that's understandable. My mom once told me my father had a choice: to run the household with discipline or love. He chose discipline based on what he saw in the classroom and his childhood experience.

The reason why this story is important is not only because it demonstrates learned parental traits but it also underscores the situational adoption of a parenting model. The generation my dad saw below him changed his parenting approach. Like it or not, my fatherhood experience was an authoritarian example. Although this style was the parental foundation I experienced, my dislike for this approach drove me to adopt an alternate style. When I became a father, I had to consciously suppress the learned behavior I experienced and try to model other parenting styles, such as the authoritative style. Even with full attention and effort in the early days, I would find myself slipping into the authoritarian style I had experienced. Luckily, my determination to be more authoritative, while incorporating all the positive values, beliefs, and traditions I experienced growing up, helped me find my sweet spot.

To some degree, I believe all parents evolve and find their style. What about your parenting style? Are you the mirror image of your parents? Are you the polar opposite or a mixture of styles? Fortunately, we aren't predisposed to default to our parents' parenting style. As you will see, multiple other influences shape how we act and raise our children. These are called our parenting influences.

Parenting Influences

We established that your parents and their parenting style can significantly impact your parenting foundation. If we take a broader perspective, your parents only form part of the picture. The second way your parenting foundation is formed is through observing and adopting what other observable mothers and fathers are doing. Frankly, any parent who was or is part of your ecosystem has directly or indirectly given you insights into parenting skills or style. Growing up, you may have observed the parents of a best friend raising their family differently. Throughout your life, you have had discussions with family, friends, schoolmates, and coworkers relating experiences, hearing humorous anecdotes, or seeking advice. Your direct exposure to parenting norms has influenced and directed your actions.

Part of your journey into learning about parenting has also been passive. As you have lived your life, you have been able to take a side seat and witness, absorb, and shamelessly steal the actions and ideas of how to be a good parent from those around you. You can probably recount numerous dinners, events, or occasions, public or private, where you have witnessed both good and bad parenting. We all have experienced a child screaming in a grocery store aisle, watching an iPad at a restaurant, or having a mental breakdown at a playground. Throughout our lives, each of these moments became a conscious or subconscious teaching moment.

A best friend or other parents present during our parenting journey become educators. Your internal parental scribe has helped you learn through observation of every interaction and discussion. If you have been fortunate to have a close friend or sibling cross over into becoming a parent before you, you have gained keen insights into their development, struggles, and journey. Every conversation where they expressed a view on raising children has given you a primer into what you could or would do. You likely tapped into their hours of experience, tips, and techniques to see what they did well and learn from their mistakes. Ultimately, you build out your parenting philosophy, which becomes your parental point of view, style, and foundation.

Finally, we can't underestimate the social norms about parenting in our society and the impact of media on the role of a parent. Whether a person watches sitcoms or movies, reads books, or interacts on social media, we have had years of media and communication influencing our perspective as a parent by the time most of us become parents. There is a volume of research on the portrayal of parents and their influence in media. Most studies summarize what we already know: media depicts gender stereotypes in society, often highlighting the "traditional nuclear family" and its issues as opposed to nonconventional families and their issues. Although this trend is changing, one shouldn't underestimate parenting roles and the influence media has on defining parenting for each of us at an early age.

Beyond your parents, who or what has been your significant parenting influence? Has it been a sibling? A friend? Or was your style adopted from a book, media, or a combination of multiple things? It's a fascinating subject. We need to understand and be aware of our style as we become empty nesters because transitioning from parent-child to parent-adult allows us to shift and improve our relationships.

Your Parenting Style Today

Now that you know your parenting origins and style, are you ready to shift your perspective? When you become an empty nester, the long-standing dynamic you and your child have become accustomed to will no longer exist. Your parental duty to control, manage, oversee, and moderate your child's life decreases significantly when they move out. The impact on your child is their dependence on you managing and doing all of these things for them ends. As both of you adjust to the upcoming change, you may find this time to be both contentious and tricky. Essentially, the power dynamic between parent and child is in flux.

> **When you become an empty nester, the long-standing parent-child dynamic you and your child have become accustomed to will no longer exist.**

Can you be a permissive, authoritative, neglectful, or authoritarian parent in your child's absence?

A lot of the Empty Nest parent-child dynamic is about preparing and letting go. Many parents hang on to the continued financial support, ongoing parental oversight, and parental expectations as control mechanisms to keep their children within their grasp. As for the departing child, they often view this situation from a completely different point of view. For the departing child, the physical move represents complete freedom and control, regardless of the areas where parental support continues. This differing perspective demonstrates how keeping the same or changing the parent-child dynamic can create conflict and control issues on both sides of the equation.

Raising a child through high school underscores that you have successfully applied your dominant parenting style. I will not make the case that you must adopt a different parenting style when you become an empty nester. This may not be the case. However, when your child moves out and starts flexing and using their independence muscles, expecting and preparing for the relationship change is beneficial. Knowing this, you may want to revisit the four parenting styles and consider making the authoritative parenting style your new dominant style. Diana Baumrind, the developmental psychologist who defined the four parenting styles, has shown through her research that adult children of authoritative parents are most likely to be well-adjusted, responsible, happy, and successful. This does not mean other styles can't produce the same results, but the data supports the idea that the authoritative style is ideal.

You can't change the past and how you raised your children and practiced the styles you were most comfortable with. If you want to switch styles now, the great news is that there is still plenty of time to flex and incorporate authoritative traits. The timing is actually ideal because you are changing your parent-child dynamic by becoming an empty nester. This change should make pivoting easier. If you feel you have a good thing going and change isn't necessary, stay put and take comfort in your knowledge of the four styles. We aren't entirely done yet. There is still much to cover and be aware of as you transition into an empty nester parent.

Being an Empty Nester Is Not Learned

Separation from one's parents is a natural transition that almost every adult goes through. You certainly have experienced it but only from one perspective, that of the departing child. This is one of the strangest things about becoming an empty nester. The experience of becoming an empty nester has been hidden from you. In the most practical sense, unlike all the other parenting actions you observed firsthand growing up, you never witnessed your parents go through their Empty Nest process. By definition, it took the action of you leaving the house to create their Empty Nest status. Even the most progressive and communicative parents likely did not share their intimate feelings or potential struggles after their child left.

If your parents had a difficult time adjusting to their Empty Nest transition, it is likely they didn't want to burden you and did not share their emotional baggage. Your eighteen- to twenty-two-year-old insight probably consisted of a "we miss you" phone call where you had little awareness of your parents' Empty Nest struggles. The default perspective from parent to teen would most assuredly have been, "Everything is okay," regardless of whether it was.

Since leaving your parent's home and having your children, have you ever sat down with your parent or parents and asked them how their Empty Nest transition went? My guess is most of us have not had that conversation. In cases where we did have this conversation, I'm not sure it would produce valuable insights. This topic has generationally been undiscussed, ignored, or remains hidden.

For most people, the theme of your child leaving the home is painted in the context of newfound freedom and space for the couple or parent. The prevailing attitude toward becoming an empty nester is a positive thing. From a societal point of view, leaving the home is considered a natural progression with age. It is regarded as a normal and healthy part of children growing up. Becoming an empty nester underscores the assumption that parents quickly move on to the next stage in life. Although this view is positive and filled with good intentions, it can make someone struggling with the transition feel left out or unsupported. Imagine a parent having anxiety, feeling loss, or experiencing sadness because of their child's departure when social norms state they should be happy. To openly express these feelings to others would be almost taboo.

What is more likely is that a parent may not be comfortable exposing their emotional vulnerability as an empty nester to others. Fear that this transition might be viewed as weakness, overbearingness, or a hyper-emotional trait by others could lead one to stay silent. The result is that an individual may bottle up their emotions or potentially struggle and go through this stage alone. In the end, people may find less awareness, sympathy, and support from their family and circle of friends because the Empty Nest transition is assumed to be positive.

I hope that conversations around becoming an empty nester are taken more seriously so that the average person can learn from their parents, friends, and others, just as we do with parenting. Your parents and others may have hesitated to discuss this transition because of the parent-child relationship and how one feels about themselves is deeply personal. The Empty Nest phase of one's life is about emotions, connection, and feelings toward a child and one's well-being.

Let's close the chapter by reflecting on and analyzing our parents and parental influences. Remember, they did their best regardless of whether you got the candy bar when you screamed for it in the grocery store line. Let's focus on a critical topic: the parent-child relationship.

CHAPTER 6 KEY POINTS

- Your parenting style was likely adopted from your parents and fine-tuned through observation.

- There are four parenting styles: permissive, authoritative, neglectful, or authoritarian.

- Adult children of authoritative parents are most likely to be well-adjusted, responsible, happy, and successful versus the other parenting styles.

- You can change and modify your parenting style.

"Remember, the goal is not to raise great kids; it's to raise kids who become great adults."

—ANDY ANDREWS

CHAPTER SEVEN

Parent-Child to Parent-Adult

WHEN YOU LOOK back at your Empty Nest transition, at least two people will experience their own completely different journey. You are at the center, playing the role of parent and individual. And then your child is at their center, the one that leaves the nest and whose departure triggers this entire shift. Thus far, we have spent much time on your perspective and history. What we haven't focused on is your departing child. Since your child is physically leaving, essentially stepping away from your daily influence and control, we must explore their departure.

In this section, I will present options for you to consider maintaining and growing your relationship with your child both before and after they leave the nest. I will share my experience, actions, and plans, which will hopefully serve as examples of approaches you can take, modify, or ignore. At a minimum, my perspective will give you some context to considerations you can make.

Beyond my own recommendations, one crucial fact remains: the single most risky thing about a child moving out of the home is that, for the first time in your life, your child has the power to dictate their relationship with you.

> **The single most risky thing about a child moving out of the home is that, for the first time in your life, your child has the power to dictate their relationship with you.**

While your child has been under your roof, they have lived by your rules and routine and have been mostly compliant in living within your parameters. You have defined and dictated your child's ecosystem for the first eighteen years of their life. When your child moves out of the home, they can redefine how they live and what they do and choose their interactions with you on their terms. This dramatic shift defines the transition from parent-child to parent-adult. Because of this, your relationship with your child is important during this stage of maturity and growth.

Since we are all creatures of habit and routine, your side of the parent-child relationship will probably continue on its current course when your child moves out. However, that routine will be physically broken since they are gone. It is also likely that, with their newfound independence, your child's parent-child relationship will change from their perspective. They will move toward or test a parent-adult relationship. You would be well served to expect this. How you prepare, interact, and adjust your parenting style toward your child during this transition will define how your relationship with them evolves into adulthood. Remember the authoritative parenting style? One where a parent is supportive, nurturing, and often on the same wavelength as their children's needs. They set clear rules and listen to and consider their children's thoughts, feelings, and opinions. This type of parent is generally both flexible and understanding. If this isn't your default, this might be a good time to review and consider adopting this approach.

Before sharing what the experts advise parents to do before and when their children leave the home, I wanted to share my experience with my three children. As you read parts of my journey and struggles, I hope it allows you to form your perspective and journey. Further, it may help you build your plan for your child in chapter 16.

My Very Own Helicopter

I take no pride in admitting that I am a recovering helicopter parent. For the record, I wasn't always this way in my fatherly role of three. I was a good partner and an active father in the early years of raising my children. That said, my wife was the primary caregiver and managed the home. We had this luxury early in our childrearing because the finances and situation made sense. The cost of full-time childcare for our son compared to the salary of a new kindergarten teacher was close to breaking even. Therefore, we decided my wife would put her career on hold so that she could stay home and raise our children. I did all the things a noble partner does in this situation. I changed diapers, bathed the children, and spent my non-work hours with the children as much as possible. Additionally, I gave up fantasy football and didn't take up golf or pursue additional outside activities so I could dedicate my free time to my family. Before we start awarding me the "Father of the Year Award," I am aware that my wife did the vast majority of the day-to-day early childhood care and feeding. She deserves the trophy.

Ten years later, as our third child entered elementary school, my wife was able to return to teaching. This transition allowed me to pivot and get more involved, essentially finding my footing as a more active part of their daily life. For the most part, school-age children's lives consist of two buckets. One bucket is school, and the other is activities.

With interests such as sports, scouts, or music lessons, my children had coaches, leaders, and teachers who happily led their activities. The director, manager, and guidance counselor roles were available with the school bucket. This is where I found my opening.

When I was in school, feedback from teacher to parent or school to parent was very limited. Parent-teacher interaction consisted of a once-a-year parent-teacher conference. Academic progress consisted of twice-yearly report cards sent home via the mail. Essentially, when I was in school, academic parenting consisted of one question: "Have you finished all your homework?" Growing up, there was no active feedback loop from parent to teacher to child.

Today, from kindergarten through high school, the feedback loop and communication have dramatically changed. The schoolteacher, accessible only through a handwritten note in my day, is now accessible via email, text, and administrative portals twenty-four hours a day. With the advent of technology, all parents have unparalleled access to what and how their children are doing. With this unprecedented access comes parental expectations from the school. Teachers and administrators expect parents to know what's happening in the classroom, on campus, and with their children. Today, school classrooms, parents, teachers, and students are more connected and interdependent than ever.

Adding to this phenomenon, many middle and high schools throughout the US have implemented, pushed, and trained parents to use their mandatory school portals.

I can't say for sure if I was on my way to applying for a "helicopter parent" pilot's license at this point in my parenting journey, but the advent of the school portal turned me into a helicopter parent. I distinctly remember receiving my first daily email summary when my oldest child started sixth grade. I was astounded that the school portal detailed my son's daily homework assignments, due dates, and future test schedules, as well as daily real-time grades. Not only was all of this information at my fingertips but additional information such as attendance, teacher feedback, and activities happening on campus were also pushed to me. At first, I tried to resist reacting to both assignments and grades, but as a parent, I felt responsible, even triggered to review and discuss all the daily details the portal reported on with my children. Although I did my best to manage my reaction and involvement, the constant portal updates shaped how I saw my role as a parent. The damn portal was responsible for issuing me the helicopter pilot's license.

I am sharing this story with you because, as my children entered high school, my daily school monitoring pressure wasn't healthy for them or me. Reflecting back, I was kidding myself by thinking I was supporting them with an authoritative parenting style when this was an authoritarian move. Even then, I thought about stepping back a little and ignoring the daily updates, and I debated whether I was helping or hovering. Sometimes I told myself I didn't want my children to make the mistakes I had made. I believed I could see the forest through the trees, thinking my fifteen-year-old could not. After all, I focused on their longer-term goals (college), and yet often, I fought against teens who didn't care about their Spanish II grades. Perhaps I share this burden with every modern parent. I am lucky my children grew more self-reliant and future-focused as high school progressed. Over time, I moderated my style toward authoritative and tried to relinquish pressure while offering support. It was hard.

As each of my children reached their junior year in high school, I pivoted away from the school portal and took on the role of college guidance counselor. We looked into colleges together, worked on admission submissions, and partnered to complete the college application processes. Ultimately, their hard work paid off, despite aspects of my helicopter involvement. The pinnacle of my children's high school careers wasn't their graduation but their acceptance into a college.

Selling the Helicopter

They say one can't change the past but can change their future. When my first child was leaving for college, I recognized that a new dynamic was taking place. As his freshman year approached, I could see his need for separation, his quest for more independence, and his desire to make his own choices. My transition assessment allowed me to step back and reframe our relationship. We transitioned from parent-child dominant to "parent-child evolving," moving ever closer to parent-adult.

As each child and parent are different, so are the relation-ship and expectations each has for the other. For me, a lot happened when my son left. His departure triggered me to ponder my Empty Nest future. As each of my children went to college, I was presented with an examination of my marriage, parenting style, and the parent-child relationship. With each departure, I realized it was time to let go of the control I had wielded for so long. This meant landing the helicopter and selling their seats when they left.

**As each of my children went to college,
I was presented with an examination
of my marriage, parenting style,
and the parent-child relationship.**

You may be asking, why not just sell the helicopter instead of selling your son's seat? This is an excellent question. My thought pattern then was that I still had two children in high school who needed my support. I would love to live in a world where parents are confident that fifteen- to seventeen-year-olds make all the right decisions. My mistakes in high school, such as cramming versus studying, not seeing the importance of trying my best, and prioritizing the "now" over the "future," made me unable to turn over the scholastic reins to my children. My parental reins loosened as I learned to relax more with each subsequent child. At the same time, I wasn't quite ready to completely let go of my involvement.

I still believed that an occasional helicopter hover or in-flight instruction was more beneficial than harmful.

My Three College Negotiables

All parents have choices to make when their children leave the home. There is no commonly accepted definition of parent-child to parent-adult. I have thought a lot about what a parent-adult relationship should look like. I have considered that an eighteen-year-old isn't instantly transformed into a full-fledged adult, yet they are far from a needy child. Knowing I needed to let go of the parent-child control, I shifted my focus to help my children develop more independence through empowerment. The more I thought about the desired parent-adult relationship, the more I saw a learning opportunity for my children. I decided to use this transitional time to fix some of my past parental mistakes while further preparing my children for their adult future. Although all of these thoughts were internal to me, it was important that, no matter my decisions, my children needed to know I was always there for them with love and support.

There is an endless list of college negotiable topics, and parents and departing children should agree on expectations before a child leaves. With my children, I decided to focus on three: school and grades, finances, and communication. I consider these three topics essential for parents and their children to discuss and agree upon if they want to support a child-adult transition. Here are my stances and philosophy for each. In totality, the three examples represent a shift from my helicopter past, which allowed me to keep my promise of letting go of control while developing independence through empowerment.

School and Grades

My first big move was to give up the academic chase. I had just spent the last seven years of my school portal life monitoring test scores, helping with class choices, and actively watching weighted and unweighted GPAs. I cared deeply because I wanted my children to have as many college options as possible. For the record, I never demanded straight As or expected my children to accomplish anything above their abilities, but for seven years, I expected and reinforced that they must try their best in school. I reinforced that each step along their academic road was important in their future journey. This was my role in middle and high school. 1 was living the guidance counselor, parent-child life.

When my son left for college, I consciously dropped all expectations and involvement in his grades. Furthermore, I decided that grades in college would not be tied to anything. Grades would not be a prerequisite for continued financial support. Grades would not be a measure of my admiration. Grades were, essentially, no longer any of my business. There is a saying, Cs get degrees (in college). So why should I care about my child's grade in statistics? The only rule imposed concerning academics in college was that we would only pay for four years. I want to say that a fifth year in a school program like engineering or a situational issue where they needed more time at school would have been considered. Still, this rule was a good starting point in ensuring they stayed on top of their class choices and graduation progress.

So, how did this laissez-faire style work for my three children? My first child, Everest, did not share a single grade with me throughout his four-year academic career at the University of California, Santa Barbara. To this day, I do not know his graduation GPA; quite frankly, it's completely irrelevant. We paid for four years, and he graduated in four years. That was the deal. Honestly, it was a relief to let go of academic pressure. My second child, Grace, tended to share the grades she was proud of, like passing Organic Chemistry with a B. Occasionally, she would mention the other side of the coin in conversations, such as "This math class is brutal; I hope I pass," or "I am hanging on to a C in this lab because it's insanely hard." Again, I found it liberating to never worry about it. Grace was worrying enough on her own, as all college students should. My third daughter, Zoe, who is currently in college, is comfortable sharing her grades with me. It's nice of her to share this information, but it's entirely her choice. My thoughts were that, as long as she met the four-year rule, we would be good. This first college negotiable, in hindsight, was a great relief.

From one parent to another, if any of my helicopter past or high school grade monitoring resonates with you, my advice is to free yourself of the academic burden once your child leaves the nest. I do understand that all children and their parental needs are different. Explore options and decide what works for you.

Finance

Everyone's experience with children and money management varies greatly, including allowances, jobs, financial support, and loans. No parent-child financial situation is the same. Because no one size fits all, I can only share my story in this section. Although I'd like to believe I did a great job raising my children in almost every category, I always worried I came up short in teaching my children the actual value of money.

My parents encouraged me to get a job as early as possible when I grew up. From an early age, it was clear that I needed to earn income if I wanted particular clothes, records, a car, or to attend college. I took this advice to heart and ventured into the workforce in my early teens. I became a newspaper carrier and babysitter and found retail and service jobs as soon as possible. My experience of working and earning money helped me develop my personal and financial skills as well as a strong work ethic. However, with my children, this dynamic was flipped. My wife and I chose not to encourage our children to work and focus on making money as teens. Instead, they were encouraged to dedicate their time to academics, sports, activities, and organizations. My children's lives were very different from mine. They had a much more rigorous academic experience. Their after-school hours and weekends were fully booked with sports, activities, and friendships. Their busy schedule wouldn't have allowed time to earn much money. A big driver for the generational parenting shift was that I knew getting into a college of their choice would be harder for them than it was for me. The mantra became, "Time spent on academics and activities was better than time spent on making money."

Part of our financial parent perspective was that we never instituted an allowance for our children. They were expected to help around the home and do chores without payment. Because of this, they never really had that much money. We occasionally gave them money for a movie or to pay for something they wanted or needed if it was a reasonable request. Their only source of income was birthday money from relatives and an occasional rare babysitting gig if they had time. Although I wholly believe this was the right choice for my children at the time, and I would make the same decision today, I always felt they were missing financial literacy. I sometimes worried that the decision to have our children not work and not focus on making money would come back to haunt us. Did I miss an opportunity to teach them the value of work and money when they were young?

Fast forward to our Empty Nest journey. As I have stated before, this time could be an opportunity. Was this an opportunity to make amends and perhaps teach my children the financial lessons they had missed? When my son left for college, I had an idea. I made the decision long ago to save and support our children through college financially, but how I chose to implement this was the opportunity I needed. I thought about how I could create a financial situation where the value of money would be taught while still fully supporting my son. I devised four financial tenets for the college-bound child, which became the backbone of how I spent and managed money with my children.

The four financial tenets are:

1. **No Credit**
2. **You Manage the Money**
3. **Just Enough to Get By**
4. **The Money Drop**

Below is a brief explanation of each tenet.

1. No Credit

Many of us have learned through experience at some point in our lifetime the valuable lesson of spending money we don't have via credit. Although this is an excellent financial lesson, it's usually a painful one that could be avoided. Tenet number one, no credit, meant we would not provide our children with a credit card and would do our best to discourage them from getting a credit card. The premise was that, if we were paying for school, room, and board, why would our college students need an additional debt mechanism? This tenet supported an underlying philosophy: credit for our college students leads to spending money one doesn't have. So, no credit.

2. You Manage the Money

The second tenet was, other than the cell phone family plan and their quarterly tuition payment, we would not actively pay their bills or manage their money. Please don't interpret this as we aren't providing funds for their expenses; we were. But they are in charge of creating and managing their budget. We were very transparent before they left for college about money, the cost of school, and their finances. When executing their budget as college students, they managed all aspects of their debits and credits. They controlled their budget and needed to manage the money.

3. Just Enough to Get By

The third tenet was, in their first year of school, we would give them very little, if any, college money. Since a first-year college experience consists of dorm life where room and board are paid for, what do they need money for? We allocated a shoestring budget for essentials and sundry items, but it was bare bones. It did not include money for Starbucks, Chipotle, clothes, or entertainment. Of course, some discretionary money was within the essential bucket, but it was purposely minimal. In year two of college, when our children moved off campus into apartments, we sat down and added up rent, food, utilities, and some essential spending money to create a budget. We agreed on a monthly stipend; they knew it was theirs to stick to.

4. The Money Drop

Finally, we instituted the fourth tenet, which was an extreme budget learning exercise. We instituted a money drop. How the money drop worked was we split their annual college expenses into two chunks: the start of the school year through December and the rest of the school year (from January to June). I added up their monthly budget for each timespan; it was bare bones, and I transferred all the money to them in a lump sum. They received one deposit when they left for school and another in January, and it was all in their hands to manage. The money drop was the most frightening tenet for my children and myself.

I am proud of the four financial tenets. I am not advising any parent to implement this with their child. Our situations, finances, and children are unique and different. Some parents may be uncomfortable with these tenets, and some children might spend their entire allotment in a few weeks. But for my children, this process worked out tremendously. The four tenets not only forced each of my college-aged children to budget and become extremely financially aware, but I was finally able to right my wrongs and make sure they learned the value of money.

They learned that Starbucks is expensive because we set the monthly budget low, just enough money to get by. They knew that eating out was expensive. They each learned that buying things they don't need is a waste of money. The outcome of this decision led to each of my children learning to make their own hard financial decisions. I beamed proudly when my children talked about clipping coupons, being frugal, and engaging in value-based shopping decisions. For us, it worked.

An added financial note: at different points in time, throughout my children's college experiences, they worked a part-time job while in college. They each saw the value in earning extra money to save for things or experiences they wanted or to increase their cash-flow balance. In no way would I say my children had it hard in college. Ultimately, a college education is a financial journey. It can involve budgeting, saving, loans, grants, scholarships and debt. No matter what your individual situation is, I recommend you use this unique financial situation as a learning experience for your child. I implore you to look at their departure and next step toward independence as an opportunity for you to help them understand and build a healthy relationship with money in the way you see fit.

They each learned that buying things
they don't need is a waste of money.

Communication

The Empty Nest Syndrome solutions section "From Control to Connection" discussed communication with one's child. Remember, throughout my research, communication is the number-one suggestion for a parent to consult with their child before their departure. This topic may seem redundant, but its importance is vital to a parent-adult relationship. This section tells the story behind the philosophy I adopted for each of my children, which may be more insightful and entertaining and help you reflect on your desired approach.

When my children left the house, my approach toward ongoing communication was deliberate and hands-off. I always thought the age-old college agreement many parents implement with their children seemed like a good plan. The plan is, "Let's set up a regular time, like Sunday at 6:00 pm, to touch base." However, after speaking with the parents who entered this agreement, the plan never seemed to stick. The feedback I was told is that schedules get busy, someone forgets, and missing an appointment becomes a point of tension instead of a positive thing, a time to connect. Knowing this, I abandoned the regular check-in time concept and defaulted to a more natural communication cadence.

My position was that each of my children knew I was there for them, and if they needed help, I would support them. I also believed that this was a time for my children to be independent and grow. In that vein, I made a conscious decision to let them drive the communication with me, and I would accept their terms. This meant I wouldn't hear from them for most of their college days, especially early on, if they didn't call. Full disclosure: there were times when I reached out, left messages, and just wanted to hear their voice. My children's communication cadence changed as time passed, but as a parent, I tried to stay true to the philosophy of giving them space and independence after they departed. Although this decision worked for us, much like with grades and finances, it may not be best for other parents and their children.

This was the most challenging adjustment because there was no set plan. Looking at my three college-aged children, phone calls and communications varied greatly. It became clear that my three children each had their own "need to check in" preference, and they were drastically different.

My first child threw himself into the independent lifestyle once he was off at school and called infrequently. He was comfortable checking in via FaceTime every few weeks or sometimes longer. My second child hated talking on the phone, and I knew this about her when she left for school. I tended to initiate phone calls out of desperation periodically, while she was more likely to text updates on her life now and then. My third child was the complete opposite of her siblings. She liked to check in during downtime or while walking across campus. She calls and texts more than the other two to connect and pass the time. My sample size of three children with the same two parents, growing up in the same household, varied greatly in how much communication they were comfortable with and needed.

The flip side of the coin was the communication we needed as parents. Frankly, the word "wanted" is better than "needed." Initially, we decided the college experience was more about their needs and growth than ours, so we consciously left the decision up to them to communicate.

Sometimes, I missed them and wanted to talk but decided to give them space. Other times, I had to check in, especially after long durations with no contact. When I looked back on the decision to have no plan, I learned we actually had one. We decided on a "needs-based" approach. And since we decided to give each child some space, that decision also meant we wouldn't overcommunicate or disrupt their developmental journey.

In hindsight, we let go of parental control to keep tabs on our children. Our routine over the last eighteen years to control communication was replaced by developing a relationship where we spoke to each other when we wanted. The decision worked for us.

In hindsight, you don't know your child's preferred interaction with you until they experience separation. The same can be said for learning how you feel and what you think you will want from them. A daily, weekly, or monthly call may be much more or much less than they prefer or you prefer.

Fundamentally, communication with your child when they leave should be more about what they need than your needs as a parent. Yes, you have needs, but your child's growth and independence should come first.

Most importantly, converse with your child regarding communication and expectations. It's okay to agree on a cadence or agree to a more unstructured schedule. In the end, please communicate with your child when you want to, but remember that this is an opportunity to help them find a balance in their communication and relationship with you. It's an essential piece of the parent-adult relationship.

Lessons Learned

We have learned that you cannot change your child through an Empty Nest transition. However, you can try to understand the dynamics of what you and your child may be going through, prepare yourself for these potential changes, and take action to improve your experience while strengthening your relationships with your child. My helicopter experience was about things I tried and learned. Each example illustrates my hope that I could positively influence my children and strengthen my relationship with them.

Much of parenting is trial and error, and each of us has triumphed and failed along our parenting journey. Each experience has made us more prepared for the next experience, regardless of the outcome. My Empty Nest transition with my children was about letting go of control and doubling up on being a supportive and understanding father. Grades, finances, and communication were levers that were important to me to define, but they do not sum up what was most important during this child-focused Empty Nest journey.

My significant decision was to let go of the parent-child relationship and embrace the evolving parent-adult relationship. I hoped the new dynamic would combine all the positive aspects of our existing relationship while creating a stronger adult relationship. In the end, I believe I have this today. My relationships with my children are still evolving and perhaps will always do so. No journey is ever truly over. I am confident my adult children are on the right path, and I have faith that yours can also be.

Sticking with our parent-child to parent-adult theme, in the next chapter, we will dive into what the experts say are the top actions parents can take to prepare their child to leave the nest.

CHAPTER 7 KEY POINTS

🖊 Adjusting from a parent-child to parent-adult relationship is a big part of a parent's empty nest journey.

🖊 When your child leaves home, it is an opportunity for you to help them build skills, become independent, and learn life lessons.

🖊 As you let go of active parenting, your child may let go of their dependence on you. This is part of their growth.

"Parents are like the bow, and children are like the arrows. It's the job of the bow to let go of the arrows, even if it means they will soar away and never return."

—UNKNOWN

CHAPTER EIGHT

Pre-Launch Advice

Readiness

BEFORE WE DIVE into the expert's pre-launch advice, I want to share the single-parent perspective on their child's readiness as they leave the nest. In my survey, I asked single parents to rate their children's emotional readiness (maturity, responsibility, concerns), their practical readiness (finances, life skills, self-care management), and their overall readiness (confidence, reservations, serious concerns) when moving out of the home. As you read the survey answers,

think through your answer to the same question. I hope sharing the survey results will give you insights into your perspective. Regarding emotional readiness, 89 percent of single parents felt their children were either very or mostly emotionally prepared to transition out of the home. This was the most decisive metric across the three readiness categories (emotional, practical, and overall). The high percentage means single parents felt their pre-launch children were mature and independent and could emotionally handle being alone.

Emotionally Ready: How ready do you feel your child is/was when moving out of the home?

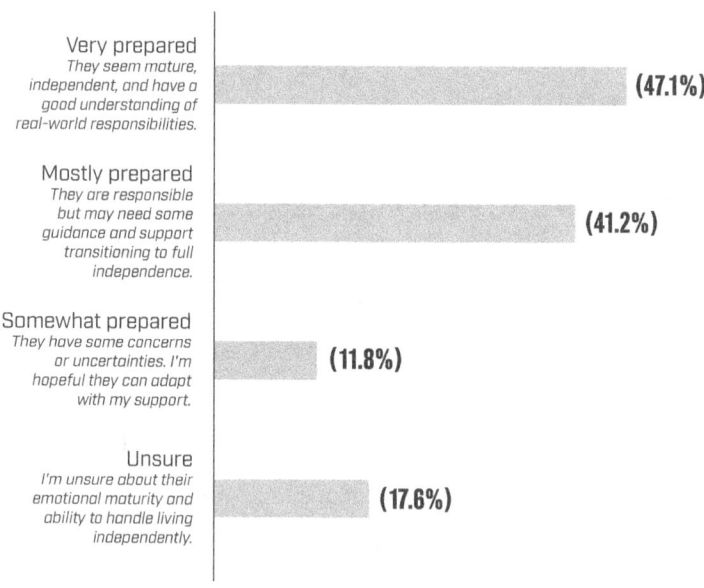

Very prepared
They seem mature, independent, and have a good understanding of real-world responsibilities. **(47.1%)**

Mostly prepared
They are responsible but may need some guidance and support transitioning to full independence. **(41.2%)**

Somewhat prepared
They have some concerns or uncertainties. I'm hopeful they can adopt with my support. **(11.8%)**

Unsure
I'm unsure about their emotional maturity and ability to handle living independently. **(17.6%)**

The percentages above can exceed 100 percent if a parent chooses to make two selections. For example, they believed their child was very prepared but felt unsure that the assessment was correct.

Regarding practical readiness, 82 percent of single parents felt their children were either entirely or well-equipped on a pragmatic basis to transition out of the home. This equates to parents feeling that their pre-launch children have the necessary survival skills. However, 17 percent felt their children had limited skills and would need more guidance and support due to lack of experience. Perhaps not surprisingly, 29 percent of single parents surveyed were worried about their child's practical readiness regardless of how prepared they felt their child was.

Practically Ready:
How ready do you feel your child is/was when moving out of the home?

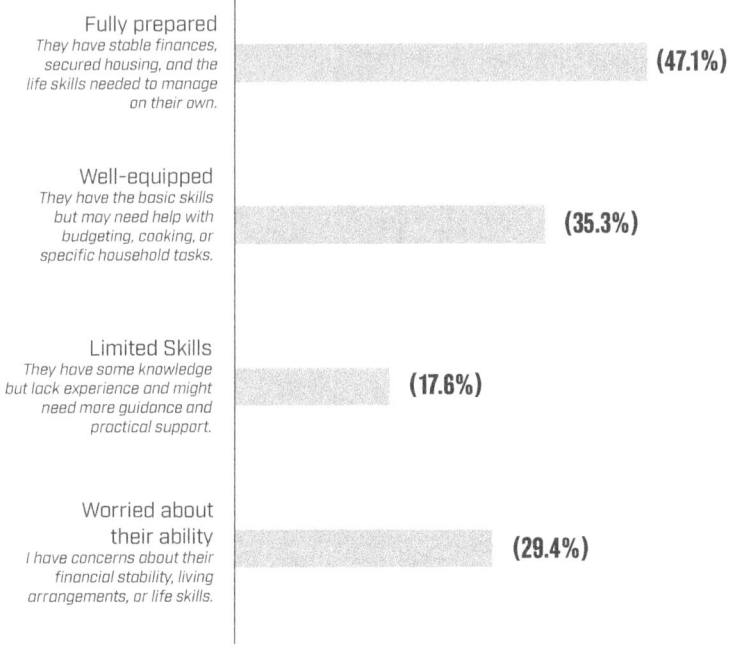

Fully prepared
They have stable finances, secured housing, and the life skills needed to manage on their own.
(47.1%)

Well-equipped
They have the basic skills but may need help with budgeting, cooking, or specific household tasks.
(35.3%)

Limited Skills
They have some knowledge but lack experience and might need more guidance and practical support.
(17.6%)

Worried about their ability
I have concerns about their financial stability, living arrangements, or life skills.
(29.4%)

When asked the higher-level question, "How ready do you feel your child is/was when moving out of the home?" the single-parent perspective remained positive but was more balanced across the top three answer categories. For example, 41 percent of single parents felt their child was completely ready, 29 percent thought they were prepared primarily, and 35 percent felt apprehensive about their child's transition. Even more positive, only 5 percent felt their child was not ready. However, for those 5 percent, which can be a large number across the entire group, this unease and concern can make this transition infinitely more stressful and anxiety-ridden.

Overall Readiness:
How ready do you feel your child is/was when moving out of the home?

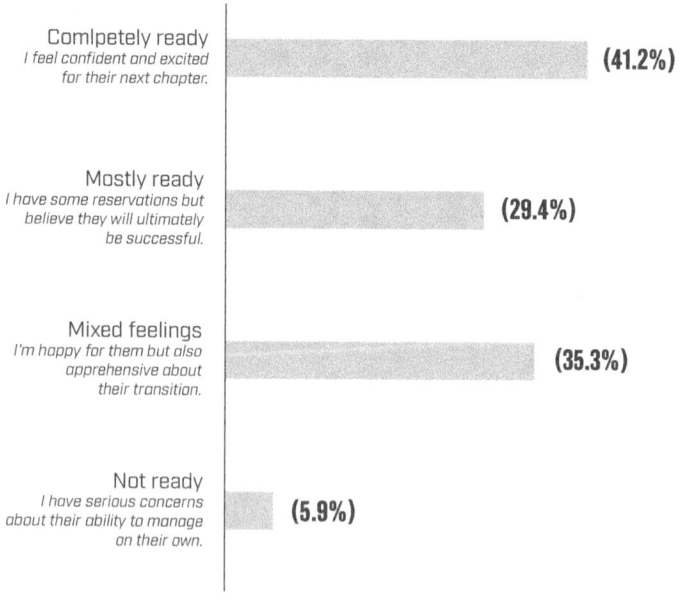

Comlpetely ready
I feel confident and excited for their next chapter. **(41.2%)**

Mostly ready
I have some reservations but believe they will ultimately be successful. **(29.4%)**

Mixed feelings
I'm happy for them but also apprehensive about their transition. **(35.3%)**

Not ready
I have serious concerns about their ability to manage on their own. **(5.9%)**

How ready is your child emotionally, practically, and overall? How do you think they will cope with their new out-of-home circumstances? As I said previously, very few children leave the nest and don't survive because they can't cook an egg or do laundry, but with independence comes some stress, anxiety, and a lot of responsibility. Let's keep that perspective in mind as we jump into pre-launch advice.

Empty Nest Preparation Advice for Your Child

Over the last two decades, you have raised your child. You have defined your parent-child relationship. You applied your preferred parenting style and watched your child's personality grow and develop. The experiences, values, and life you have provided for your child have established many of the individual traits they have today.

In the previous chapter, I detailed my experiences raising and letting go of my children. It is possible that, for some parents, nothing of consequence will change when their child moves out. A child can truly be on their own and experience living independently, making their own decisions without parental influence or actions. Parents don't have to do anything during this time other than let the child's transition take its natural course.

However, as discussed in the last several chapters, this stage in your life can be an opportunity. It can be a time for reflection, a time to set priorities, and an opportunity for change. As your parent-adult relationship starts forming, you have a chance to reestablish and redefine the relationship you have with your child. In my case, it was good to let go. It was a growth experience for me and my children and an opportunity to strengthen our relationship. For the best of parent-child dynamics, it can be an opportunity to make a great relationship even better. You can leverage all the good, embrace their independence, and help them transition into adulthood. Although there is no perfect time to start this transition, the milestone of their departure gives you a timeline to work with.

There are endless articles, blogs, and books on how to send your child off to college, the military, or on their own. There are even more articles on what children need from their parents. Most of the advice I found falls into the following two categories:

- What can you do for your child as they leave the nest?
- What can they do for themselves, set up by you?

The majority of the advice I found fell into six themes for both parents and children:

1. **Staying connected**
2. **Finding balance**
3. **Defining rules and expectations**
4. **Preparing them for Independent Living**
5. **Using support structures**

6. **Resolving conflicts**

Below, I have summarized the advice and suggestions I researched with my perspective sprinkled in.

1. Staying Connected

Although this topic is covered peripherally in both the Empty Nest Syndrome solutions section and the last section, it still merits additional thought. To avoid redundancy, the overall premise is to talk with your child before they leave about their preference or expectations around ongoing communication. During this conversation, you can also communicate what you want from them. This will be a one-sentence discussion for some parents because they know their child will reach out if necessary or their child is an active communicator. For others, the discussion should happen so that an uncommunicative parent or child can express needs and hopefully align.

In all that I have read, when there are communication differences and differing expectations about frequency and content between child and parent, stress, resentment, and cracks in the relationship can occur. The only way to prevent adverse outcomes from happening is to have the conversation upfront. My advice is to come from a place of "we love you, and we will miss you" when bringing this subject up, so positivity is the basis for the discussion. In my experience, the communication dynamic will find its rhythm. If this doesn't happen out of the gate, it will most likely fall into place after a few months when your child is finished being overwhelmed and preoccupied with independence and settled into a routine.

2. Finding Balance

Part of your child's journey into independence, maturity, and responsibility is letting them make decisions on their own. This means you need to give them some space. As discussed in the Empty Nest Syndrome solutions chapter, this can be when the habit of hyper-connectivity and dependence on either a parent or the child can be adjusted.

I advise the hyper-communicative parent to stop calling and texting constantly and be more measured with your outreach to your child. Part of their growth will depend on you pulling back. One way to look at it is to be there for them when they need you but don't depend on them for your daily debriefing fulfillment.

For the hyper-communicative child, try to find a balance between letting them figure things out independently while exploring relationships and dependence on their peers. You should not always be at their beck and call for everything. This can be easier said than done. You are not obliged to pick up every call, call or text them back immediately, or solve all their problems. Since all parent-adult relationships are different, the summary advice is to do a sanity check for balance. Balance your communication, and remember this is a time for your child's personal growth and independence.

3. Defining Rules and Expectations

Remember the authoritative parenting style? As you now know, it is considered the best style for raising a well-adjusted, responsible, happy, and successful child. The first part of the authoritative parenting style definition states, "Parents set clear rules; they listen to and take into consideration their children's thoughts, feelings and opinions." Just because your child leaves the home doesn't mean there are no more extended rules or expectations. In summary, rules list what one should and should not do. We all live by rules. Expectations communicate a desired behavioral outcome. For example, "I expect you to pass your classes." Finally, there is advice. Advice is not a rule or expectation but the wisdom you hope your child will adopt. A piece of advice I gave my children was, "Always attend class at school. Most professors test what they teach in class."

Advice is not a rule or expectation
but the wisdom you hope
your child will adopt.

By now, your rules and values have been ingrained in your child. They know and understand what you believe is right and wrong. You may only need to reinforce a few rules at this stage in their life before they leave the nest. A practical example would be, "Your car is only insured for you as a driver; therefore, don't let friends borrow or drive your car." Beyond a few rules, parents are more inclined to offer advice before their child leaves. For example, "Make sure you take a buddy out with you if you go out at night." As parents, we have a lot of advice about safety and being responsible. You can't rely on rules, so parting wisdom as advice may be more likely to stick with a departing child. My advice from one parent to another is, "Keep rules to a minimum." See how I offered advice and downplayed rules?

Expectations we have for our children are their own unique thing. Stepping back, we all have expectations as parents, children, employees, and students. Expectations can include financial, social, academic, personal care, etc. If you stop and think about it, your expectations for your child are endless. You expect them to be kind, get enough sleep, be good drivers, eat well, and be happy. The list goes on and on. When it comes to expectations you have when they leave the home, I recommended you think through and narrow down your expectations to a top few. After you have your top expectations list, you will have a profound yet casual conversation with your child about what they are and why you have them.

For my three children, my top expectations were:

- Show up for class.
- Take school seriously.
- Graduate in four years.

These expectations weren't new to them, and I communicated them over time and in different ways. I probably said something like the following or pieces of the following for years when discussing my own experience in college: "Going away to college is both a privilege and a great opportunity for you. I want you to get the most out of your four years and have fun. Think of college as your full-time job. My recommendation is to show up for class. Many college students blow off classes, struggle, and fall behind. If you show up consistently, you will be doing yourself a favor by being ahead of the others regarding test preparation. I trust you to make the most of this time and do your best." See how I weaved my three expectations in there?

To be clear, I also wanted my children to eat healthy, not binge drink, brush their teeth, and drive safely. I wanted all of those things. However, I viewed this as an opportunity to underscore the responsibility they were taking on when they went off to college and not the kitchen sink of all expectations and advice.

Your child likely has expectations of you. I didn't implicitly ask my children what their expectations were of us; perhaps that was a missed opportunity. I would encourage you to have that conversation if you can make it natural and get something out of it. There were implied expectations and requests for my children without the formal sit-down. For example, we were expected to pay for school and the cost of living. They expected that we would help them move into college and supply them with the necessities they needed on move-in day. We were expected to come to Parent's Weekend and visit them on campus. Although these and other expectations weren't necessarily discussed beforehand, they were assumed or mentioned as time passed. My final point is that, in a parent-adult relationship, as with any relationship, expectations go both ways.

4. Preparing Them for Independent Living

No late-teen to early twenty-year-olds ever died because they couldn't cook an egg or do laundry. At least, not that I am aware of. Since we all come from different cultures and each of our children has been uniquely raised, every young adult leaving home will have a wide variety of skills they have mastered and things they have never done (i.e., cooking that egg or doing laundry). All articles on this subject suggest that parents try to arm their children with basic day-to-day self-care survival skills to make their transition into independent living as painless as possible. The basic skills often mentioned include shopping, food preparation, laundry, finances, cleaning, and personal hygiene. Countless activities and skills are needed for independent living; hopefully, your child has mastered many.

Articles suggest parents quickly inventory what their child knows and may need to know and then take the time to teach them a few vital skills before they leave. Some articles I have read go into greater depth and mention teaching children to set alarms and wake up, manage taking prescription drugs, or review the "dos and don'ts" of living with a roommate. Skills cited essential for young adults include time management, healthy habits, stress management, and mental health. Each of these skills can fall under the self-care umbrella. It's important to remember that self-care is ongoing and can look different for each child. Even something as simple as reading emails was mentioned as a necessary skill with the explanation that many professors communicate via email while many children today do not.

As parents sending our children off to college, we know the skills our children were proficient in, and we were also aware of some gaps. Basic skills are what one needs to know for dorm or apartment living. Ultimately, your child will survive and figure things out with or without your teaching. But if you believe they should change their sheets more than once a school year, some basic 101 lessons aren't wrong.

5. Using Support Structures

Most schools today do an excellent job in new student orientation, letting them know the free services and support available on campus. Professors and academic advisers recommend going to office hours and signing up for free tutoring if there is a need for educational help. Each school proactively encourages using the student medical center or student health services if health or personal issues arise. There are layers and layers of support available for most college students if they take the initiative, ask for help, and know where to look.

If you have attended a college orientation or tour with your child, you know that most schools throw a lot of information at parents and students in a very short amount of time. Although all the support structures and benefits are communicated, I recommend keeping them in mind as a parent. If your child experiences hardships, you can point them in the right direction versus taking on the problem and troubleshooting issues yourself. On the same theme, if your child is heading into the workplace instead of college, they also have a support structure. Most jobs set expectations with their employees and have managers and HR departments available to answer questions, and employees can always tap into more experienced peers at their work to troubleshoot issues or answer questions. Resources are usually available for almost anything if one knows where to look.

While at college, our three children used free tutoring services, visited the medical center, and took advantage of their professors' office hours. They each leveraged the different benefits that came with school tuition. Gyms, career centers, student services, academic advisers, and the library were just some of the benefits they each used. Workplace and educational institutions have built various support structures and benefits waiting to be used and often underutilized. I advise your child to be aware of the benefits they are entitled to and proactively use them when needed.

6. Resolving Conflicts

One of the major, if not the primary, recommendations to parents and children during this time is to attempt to resolve any outstanding relationship issues and conflicts before move-out day. Many of the problems and conflicts mentioned with this warning center on expectation setting, specifically clarifying expectations around finances, independence, lifestyle, grades, etc. Since we already covered expectations, let's focus on the interpersonal issues and conflicts that were mentioned the most.

Moving out of the house can be stressful for both parent and child. Many articles say to expect temper flare-ups, arguments, and emotional ups and downs from both child and parent. The first general advice is to be aware of and anticipate this. Some parents seem to struggle to adjust to the upcoming loss of control and worry about their child's departure. Departing children, on the other hand, often test boundaries and flex their independence with their parents as their departure approaches. On the emotional side, departing children usually deal with their friend group departing and are equally nervous about their departure.

The key for you as a parent is to anticipate this behavior and these feelings and be prepared not to overreact while being sympathetic to your child. Understanding that familial tension during this time is quite normal can relieve some of the mystery and drama. Most articles also state that when a conflict occurs, such as failing grades, running out of money, or roommate issues, try to remain calm and think through the best path forward versus focusing on who is right and wrong or conveying disappointment. One article from Healthy Children.org states, "Fights don't solve problems; they make new ones." Try to put yourself in the same situation as your child and consider how you would like the conflict resolved fairly.

> **Understanding that familial tension during this time is quite normal can relieve some of the mystery and drama.**

Much of parent-child conflict resolution falls into the category of parenting 101. Luckily, you have been practicing this skill throughout your child's life. The significant distinction now is to understand that you are transitioning to a parent-adult relationship where terms such as "because I said so" will no longer be acceptable. Adding to the complexity of this transitional time, your child may be physically away when issues arise and can hang up, walk away, or ignore you if things get hot. Because of this, it is in your best interest to work through conflict and deescalate emotions calmly.

The top recommended suggestions for resolving issues and conflicts are to be open with your feelings, apologize if you are wrong, and try to seek to understand the conflict or issue from your child's perspective. If you can remain respectful and calm and work toward a resolution when faced with conflict, you will be doing yourself and your child a huge favor. As parents, we know this is easier said than done, but part of your Empty Nest journey is to grow and evolve your relationships and yourself.

Summary Advice

Two general themes came up repeatedly in my research that I wanted to paraphrase and distill into advice. The first piece of advice is for you, the parent, to relate to your child. Be confident in your child's newfound independence and encourage them that they are ready for this next phase in their life. If your child sees that you believe in them and their abilities, they will be more confident and prepared to succeed independently. The second recommendation is to remind yourself that you have raised your child well. You have instilled values, taught them lessons, and helped them build their character and the foundation of who they are today. They are equipped with all the tools you have already given them, which they can use to succeed. Both of these recommendations serve as a way to reinforce to your child and yourself that this transition will be okay.

At its core, this book is about the Empty Nest journey, which centers around you. As I have said, thousands of books on children, parenting, and relationships go into much greater detail and provide sound advice. Because your Empty Nest journey also involves your child, this book wouldn't have been complete without discussing your child and addressing their role in your experience.

In the next chapter, we will explore the threats and worst-case scenarios for parents entering this stage in their lives. The Empty Nest Threats outline future issues that parents may face and bring light to problems that may already be in motion. By exploring the threats, we will understand how and why they happen, enabling us to pivot and embrace the Empty Nest Opportunities.

CHAPTER 8 KEY POINTS

- Preparing your child to leave the nest is about more than ensuring they have enough underwear.

- There are six recommended areas on which you can focus your pre-launch preparation: staying connected, finding balance, defining rules and expectations, preparing them for independent living, using support structures, and resolving conflicts.

- Out of all the recommended pre-launch focus areas, experts underscore that resolving conflicts is vital to ensuring a healthy parent-adult relationship.

"I'm a single parent. What's your superpower?"

— ANONYMOUS

CHAPTER NINE

The Uniqueness of Being a Single Empty Nester

On Our Own

THE MAJORITY OF information on being an empty nester can apply to either a single or married parent. Any individualized situations, understanding, or emotions are unique to that parent's experience. However, the experience of raising a child by yourself, making decisions independently, and being

a solo parent comes with challenges and advantages unique to a single parent. Having a partner share in the responsibilities of child-raising and decision-making while being a co-supporting influence is an entirely different parenting experience than parenting on one's own. This book is not about how to be a single parent; however, when the single parent is on the verge of becoming an empty nester, I think it is essential to review the most common challenges and advantages a single empty nester may face versus their married counterpart. The following two sections were compiled from personal interviews, surveys, articles, and data on the subject. They are not an all-inclusive list of inevitable challenges and advantages all single empty nesters experience; they are the most common points based on my research.

Challenges

Here is a summarized list of seven challenge categories, in no particular order, that single empty nesters experience when their child leaves home:

1. **Loneliness:** After years of having a child be a present and constant force in one's life, single parents may experience loneliness when their child leaves home. They can miss their child's companionship, support, and household noise. Unsurprisingly, single parents may experi-

ence this more intensely than parents in two-parent households, as their child has been an emotional confidant and source of comfort. The loss of this support can be challenging.

2. **Emotional and Mental Health:** The stress of parenting alone, coupled with potential feelings of isolation, can take a toll on a single empty nester's emotional well-being. Single empty nesters may have historically not prioritized self-care and maintaining physical and mental well-being. Additionally, they might feel anxiety and depression due to not only a historical lack of time for socializing but also difficulties finding people who understand their situation.

3. **Financial Challenges**: Single parents often have to manage the family's finances independently, which can be challenging with a single income. When a child leaves home, the single parent may have to adjust their budget to cover the increased living costs on their own, especially if the child was contributing to the household income, or they could be now supporting two separate households, their own and their child's. Education, room and board, and transportation are cited as full or partial additional expenditures. Several single empty nesters mentioned that long-term planning and saving on a single income was challenging.

4. **Parenting Teenagers as They Enter Adulthood**: Teenagers can be challenging for a parent even when two parents are in the household. Single parents may find it even more challenging to deal with older teenage rebellion and handle all parenting decisions, mood swings, and discipline. One single parent mentioned, "There are no two against one or good cop/bad cop; it's just me policing on my own."

5. **Dating and Relationships**: Some single empty nesters mentioned they found it difficult to date and form new relationships after their child left, because they spent most of their free time with or focusing on their child. Single empty nesters often mentioned that they feel they don't have enough time or energy to devote to a new partner due to them still figuring things out for themselves. Some had negative opinions toward "dating today" and were overwhelmed with online dating or navigating an unknown hook-up culture.

6. **Adjusting to a New Routine**: Although a new routine is present in a married and single household when a child leaves home, a single parent's entire routine will likely change without the commonality or stability of a partner and a child. Adjusting to newfound free time and determining how to fill it can be challenging. Additionally, maintaining social connections and avoiding withdrawal may be difficult without the routine and dependence

on school events and child-based activities. Several single empty nesters stated they struggled to reestablish a social life around their child.

7. **Finding a New Purpose in Life**: After years of being focused on raising their child, single parents may need to find a new purpose in life. A single empty nester may be reassessing their identity outside of their role as a parent, which can lead to a sense of purposelessness. The transition to being alone and only having work, for example, to occupy one's time may create a more dramatic need to rediscover new interests and goals.

These examples mention a recurring warning that, when a single parent makes a decision, takes action, or comes up with a perspective on any situation by themselves, the weight of the process is challenging. One single empty nester stated, "There is no blaming anyone else for a good or bad decision. All parenting decisions I made point back to me… there is stress that comes with being the sole decision maker." Many of these topics were mentioned repeatedly by single empty nesters.

Advantages

It should come as no surprise that single empty nesters also see the benefits of being the sole decision maker and a single point for all things parenting. Many challenges also had an opposing argument as an advantage. For example, some single parents stated they struggled to make significant life and big decisions concerning their children independently. At the same time, it was mentioned repeatedly that making a decision quickly and independently was viewed as a blessing or a strength. Survey responses such as, "I don't have to barter or debate with anyone. If I'm confident with a choice, I make it." were common.

Here is a summarized list of nine advantages, in no particular order, that many single empty nesters embrace when their child leaves home:

1. **Independence and Autonomy**: Single parents have more practice with independence and unconstrained decision-making. Having complete control over household decisions, routines, and lifestyle choices without negotiating with a partner is an advantage. Single parents may also have more opportunities to rediscover and embrace their independence and autonomy once their children leave the nest. Some single parents pointed out that the transition into empty nesting may be less jarring because they are already used to managing the household independently.

2. **Flexible Lifestyle**: Single parents may find it easier to adapt to a more flexible lifestyle, as they no longer have to coordinate schedules and responsibilities

with a spouse and children. There are no negotiating changes to routines or schedules but rather the ability to adapt to their desires freely. To that end, freedom and spontaneity were mentioned repeatedly when speaking about having the flexibility to travel, pursue hobbies, or change plans on a whim without the constraints of parenting responsibilities.

3. **Personal and Professional Growth**: The Empty Nest phase for a single parent provides a chance for personal growth and self-discovery, as they have more time and space to focus on their interests and aspirations. Many single empty nesters felt they could invest time and resources in their education, personal development, or career advancement without competing priorities.

4. **Financial Freedom**: Although two working parents statistically allow for greater pooling of finances and more financial stability for a couple, some single empty nesters stated that their financial dependencies related to children decreased after they left home, which came with several benefits. The most stated benefits included financial decisions becoming less complicated, a greater sense of economic freedom, and an ability for more personal spending.

5. **Social Connections**: Without spousal or child-related social commitments, many single empty nesters cited more time and energy to invest

in social relationships, friendships, and community involvement. Being able to give undivided attention or support to previously semi-neglected support systems like friends, family, or new social circles meant that reinvesting in relationships both increased and strengthened.

6. **Reduced Stress**: Some single empty nesters mentioned that decreased day-to-day responsibilities associated with parenting and household teenage drama reduced overall stress levels. Additionally, not having to manage a partner's day-to-day emotions allowed them to focus solely on their well-being.

7. **Rekindling Relationships**: Single empty nesters may have the opportunity to rekindle or explore new romantic relationships without the same level of family obligations or relationship complications. One parent stated, "It's dating without compromise; I can enter the dating world at my own pace and on my terms." Many single parents surveyed planned on returning to the dating scene once their child left.

8. **Health and Wellness**: With more time to focus on self-care, single empty nesters may experience improvements in their overall health and well-being. Some single empty nesters saw the transition as an opportunity to change habits and become more resilient. In contrast, others emphasized that they already had good self-care strategies to cope with

change, more self-care practice, and more resilience
experience. Both groups saw this transition as
a health and wellness opportunity.

9. **Co-Parent Struggles**: Unlike married couples,
    single empty nesters don't experience child-leaving
    and spouse-role changes simultaneously. Some
    stated they could form a deeper connection
    with the remaining children without managing
    a partner's relationship dynamics. Less competition
    for attention in the household led to building more
    robust, more independent relationships with their
    departing and remaining children.

The contradiction between the challenges and advantages
proves that every coin has two sides. We would be doing
a disservice to all single empty nesters if we applied these
contrasting points of view as just being "in the eye of the
beholder." One parent's experience during the Empty Nest
transition could easily equate to financial pressure, debt, and
worry while another may experience fewer monthly expenses
and reduced personal stress. These lists allow us to reflect on
our situation and perhaps gain empathy, understanding, and
perspective on the other side of the coin. Let's apply these
examples to you personally.

Exercise 1—You

Directions: You have reviewed the challenges and
advantages of being a single empty nester. Let's review

each again and create your scorecard. You likely did this mentally while reading each example, but seeing them in totality may help you form an overall viewpoint. Put a checkmark next to the advantage and challenge you have experienced/identified with.

ADVANTAGES	✓	CHALLENGES	✓
Independence and Autonomy (Decision Making)		Loneliness	
Flexible Lifestyle (Freedom and Spontaneity)		Emotional and Mental Health	
Personal and Professional Growth		Financial Challenges	
Financial Freedom		Parenting Teenagers as They Enter Adulthood	
Social Connections		Dating and Relationships	
Reduced Stress		Adjusting to a New Routine	
Rekindling Relationships		Finding a New Purpose in Life	
Health and Wellness			
Co-Parent Struggles			

How'd you do? Do you have more challenges or more advantages? Did any of them surprise you? Are some understandably contradicting? And finally, and most importantly, are there some advantages where you don't have a checkmark and could focus time and energy on and create one? As we can see, the challenges are all based on the past. If you have a checkbox following a challenge, this has happened to you. These are the challenges you have faced and may still be facing.

Let's turn our focus to the advantages. The advantages may not be as cut and dried. Many of the benefits are personal perspectives or outlooks. Regardless of whether you have experienced many advantages, you can review the list and work toward creating them in the future. We will do this when you make your plan for yourself in chapter 15.

Review your advantages and choose the three to five most important and meaningful to you.

Example:

MY ADVANTAGES	✓
Independence and Autonomy	✓
Flexible Lifestyle	✓
Social Connections	✓
Health and Wellness	✓

Your three to five choices underscore what you value, want, and wish to do moving forward. These are your Empty Nest advantages. Each is important to you for a very personal reason. They may be habits you practice or goals you wish to accomplish. Either way, your list should reinforce what you can and want to embrace moving forward on your empty nesting journey.

Broader Challenges

Before we move on to the Empty Nest Threats in the next chapter, I want to discuss the elephant in the room. Single empty nesters face many challenges as a group in the United States. By the time this group reaches the Empty Nest phase, they will likely have endured many more financial and social hardships than their married counterparts. As I stated earlier, most of the data on this group is reported on parents with children from birth to eighteen years old. After a single parent is no longer actively parenting or their child becomes an eighteen-year-old adult, government surveys, financial data, and our understanding of this group statistically disappear. It is as though a single parent drops their parenting title and sta-tistically becomes bundled into the group called single adults in the United States. Unfortunately, statistics on single adults in the US drown out the unique single-parent data.

This book focuses on everything related to the Empty Nest transition for parents forty-four to sixty-five years old. It purposely does not examine single parents' hardships for the first eighteen years of their parenting life. However, I would feel remiss if I didn't highlight the broader challenges and statistics related to this group. You, the single parent, may identify with some of the difficulties mentioned, or you may not. Regardless, I want to acknowledge that many single parents, and potentially single empty nesters, faced additional challenges besides the list we previously examined. FinancesOnline.com compiled the following bullet points in an article titled, *45 Single Parent Statistics You Can't Ignore: 2024 Gender, Race & Challenges.*

- 'Single parent statistics census shows that single-parent families struggle with poverty, with single mothers being in a worse position than single fathers.'
- Three in five poor children in the US (60%) lived in families headed by unwed mothers. This is a poverty rate of 31%, while those headed by an unwed father had a poverty rate of 15%. The lowest poverty rate is 5% for families headed by a married couple. (National Women's Law Center, 2020)
- The poverty rate for families of unmarried mothers who are of color is highest among Native Americans at 43%. This is followed by unmarried mothers who are African American (35%), Latino (34%), non-Hispanic White (26%), and Asian (22%). (National Women's Law Center, 2020)
- On average, single-parent households spend 34% of their household income on child care. On the other hand, families usually spend over 10% of their household income on child-care costs for a single child. (CNBC, 2020)

- Single parents reported higher levels of stress (59.1%) in 2020 compared to parents from other households (53.4%). They also reported higher levels of anxiety (43.2%), depression (35.1%), and loneliness (54.9%) compared to parents from other households. (Center for Translational Neuroscience at the University of Oregon, 2020)
- Out of all household expenses, single-parent households had the most difficulty in paying for utilities (56.5%), followed by housing (50.6%), then food (46.7%). (Center for Translational Neuroscience at the University of Oregon, 2020)
- Single-parent households were more likely to cut back spending overall (73.5%), postpone in-person healthcare visits to doctors and hospitals (62.1%), and cancel summer trips or camps (50.3%). (Liberty Street Economics, 2020)

I hate to close out a chapter on a sad note, but the data and statistics don't lie. Some single parents start in poverty, others situationally struggle, and others do not have financial difficulties. Additionally, mental and physical health is a concern for single parents as well as the general population. I want to acknowledge that single parents as a collective group struggle financially and face hardships. If there is a bright side to point to, it is that the happiness that children bring and the benefits of being a parent cannot be measured in monetary terms despite the costs and struggles of raising a child. As a result, despite the sporadic roadblocks, being a single parent can be seen as a success in and of itself. Perhaps Meg Lowrey put it best: "Being a single parent is not a life full of struggles but a journey for the strong."

"Being a single parent is not a life full of struggles but a journey for the strong."

In the next chapter, we will explore the Empty Nest threats and worst-case scenarios for parents entering this stage in their lives. The Empty Nest Threats outline future issues that parents may face and bring light to problems that may already be in motion. By exploring the threats, we will understand how and why they happen, enabling us to pivot and embrace the Empty Nest Opportunities.

CHAPTER 9 KEY POINTS

- Being a single empty nester comes with its unique challenges and advantages

- There are seven summarized challenges and nine advantages to being a single empty nester.

- Your three to five Empty Nest advantages reinforce what you can and wish to embrace moving forward

- Single parents as a group in the United States have more financial and mental health-related challenges than their married counterparts.

"You know your children are growing up when they stop asking you where they came from and refuse to tell you where they're going."

—P.J. O'ROURKE

CHAPTER TEN

Empty Nest Threats

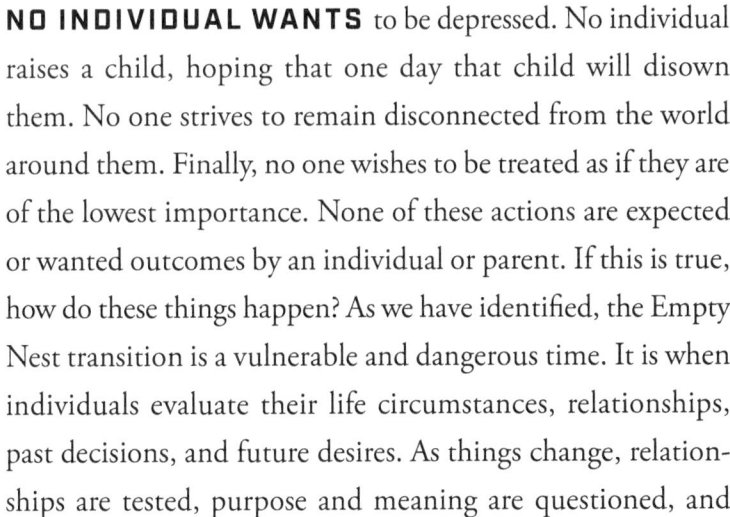

NO INDIVIDUAL WANTS to be depressed. No individual raises a child, hoping that one day that child will disown them. No one strives to remain disconnected from the world around them. Finally, no one wishes to be treated as if they are of the lowest importance. None of these actions are expected or wanted outcomes by an individual or parent. If this is true, how do these things happen? As we have identified, the Empty Nest transition is a vulnerable and dangerous time. It is when individuals evaluate their life circumstances, relationships, past decisions, and future desires. As things change, relationships are tested, purpose and meaning are questioned, and

realizations about oneself are made. There are Empty Nest Threats that come with this transition in life, which single empty nesters may wish to avoid.

The Single Parent Empty Nest Threats are depression, disownment, disconnection, and deprioritization. I will refer to these threats as the four Ds. As we will explore in this chapter, the first three Ds can sneak up on a single parent regardless of whether they are a current or future empty nester. The routine-based functioning household, where a parent is busy focusing on their children, will completely change when the last child departs. The departure catapults both the child into a new circumstance and the parent into a new reality of individual focus. Personal happiness, companionship, and future needs are just some common themes that come into question under this circumstance. Put another way, if there are gaps, issues, or vulnerabilities in a parent-child relationship or an individual's sense of self, an Empty Nest transition can bring about Empty Nest Threats. Throughout this chapter, we will explore the three Ds and discover how each can rear its head as our Empty Nest transition comes to fruition. After reading this chapter, I hope you will have become more aware of the first three Empty Nest Threats and, more importantly, be ready to do what it takes to conquer them.

D #1—Depression

Depression is an internally focused state. It is an experience one has with themselves that can be debilitating during this stage in one's life. This category is called depression, but we will also include many of the negative emotions single parents experience during their Empty Nest transition. Depression is classified as a mood disorder. It may be described as sadness, loss, or anger that interferes with a person's everyday activities. Contrast that definition with Empty Nest Syndrome's definition: "a parent or parents who are feeling a sense of loss, grief, and sadness when their child leaves the home." The two are remarkably similar. Additionally, both depression and Empty Nest Syndrome can be short-lived or continue indefinitely and seem to impact parents globally regardless of race, economic status, or country. To ground ourselves on the topic of depression, let's look at some statistics on the frequency of depression and which age ranges seem to be most susceptible.

DEPRESSION IN THE UNITED STATES OF AMERICA (OVER TWO WEEKS)
2019 Survey—Centers for Disease Control and Prevention

- 18.5% of American adults (roughly 1 in 5) had symptoms of depression.
- 11.5% experienced mild symptoms.
- 4.2% experienced moderate symptoms.
- 2.8% experienced severe symptoms.

EXPERIENCING DEPRESSION BY AGE RANGE
2019 Survey—Centers for Disease Control and Prevention

adults experiencing symptoms of depression
- 21.0%—aged 18-29
- 16.7%—aged 30-44
- 18.5%—aged 45-64
- 18.4%—aged 65 and over

Interestingly, the second-highest age group of adults suffering from depression falls into the Empty Nest timeline. Equally as concerning is the number-one age group suffering from depression, which is the age range of most departing children. Additionally, the study pointed out that the forty-five to sixty-four-year-old age group was the leading age group experiencing moderate depression. In contrast, the percentage of adults who experienced severe depression symptoms did not vary significantly by age.

What's clear across the board is that a significant number of people in the United States are dealing with some form of depression, and the Empty Nest age range and the age range of departing children are unfortunately right in the mix. Before I throw the term depression around any further, I'd like to break down the differences between situational depression and clinical depression. This is important because it will help you better contextualize the type of depression the Empty Nest age group may be going through.

Situational and Clinical Depression

A stressful or traumatic event causes **situational depression**. Symptoms may be similar to symptoms of clinical depression but are usually more short-lived in a reaction to the event. For example, an upsetting or stressful life event might be losing one's job, divorce, illness, money worries, death of a parent, or adjusting to a child leaving the home.

Clinical depression is a more chronic condition that is severe enough to interfere with daily function. It is described as someone being in a constant sense of hopelessness and despair, which gets in the way of one's life for an extended period. There are many causes for depression, which can lead to clinical depression ranging from biological to circumstantial. Some examples of clinical depression triggers are brain chemistry, family history, early childhood trauma, and chronic pain.

Situational depression can often improve over time as an individual recovers from the feelings associated with the stressful event. However, in cases where situational depression goes on for a long time and is left untreated, it can turn into clinical depression.

Empty Nest Depression

Becoming an empty nester, coming to terms with one's new life and potentially a new status, and dealing with parental adjustment can impact an individual emotionally. Most parents have had the opportunity to influence their children's daily lives profoundly, so the loss of connectivity, availability, and dependency can trigger many emotions and feelings. Some of those feelings fall under the definition of situational depression.

An Empty Nest parent can experience guilt, grief, loneliness, sadness, and abandonment when their child departs the home. The feelings of loss (of self, purpose, meaning, and drive) are also often associated with a parent going through an Empty Nest transition. Some situational feelings and emotions can be mild and pass quickly while others may linger throughout a more extended adjustment phase.

Although none of these feelings are inevitable, a parent may deal with multiple negative emotions in an Empty Nest Threat scenario. What is socially accepted as a joyous time of personal growth as one's child launches into the world can be emotionally challenging for a parent. If there is a hidden victim in this transition, it is the parent, as all the attention and celebration is usually directed toward the departing child.

If there is a hidden victim in this transition, it is the parent, as all the attention and celebration is usually directed toward the departing child.

Throughout this book, when sadness, loneliness, and depression are mentioned in the context of an Empty Nest, the examples used have centered on a parent's negative emotions felt after a child's departure. Although this is perhaps the default scenario, positive milestones can also lead to depression. For example, the most decorated Olympic swimmer in history with twenty-eight medals, Michael Phelps, has openly discussed his bouts with severe anxiety and major depression he felt after every Olympic game he participated in. In a 2022 interview with *Healthline*, an online health information site, Phelps said, "[You] work so hard for four years to get to that point, and then it's like you're… at the top of the mountain. You're like, what the hell am I supposed to do? Where am I supposed to go? Who am I?" These questions are similar to what an Empty Nest parent may ask themselves. The goal of an Olympic medal or successfully rearing and launching a child out of the nest does not grant you immunity from depression. In fact, it can cause it.

A parent experiencing negative emotions during their Empty Nest transition may find the negativity compounding if they feel they are alone without a support structure or societal understanding. Combine this situational depression or emotional challenge with additional outside stresses such as menopause, job insecurity, health concerns, or other harmful external factors, and one could quickly become depressed. Depression can have a profound impact on a person's mental and physical health as well as their personal and professional relationships. This is a threat that empty nesters should be aware of and potentially try to mitigate by seeking support through others or professional help. Most worrisome would be if any of these situations and feelings continued over time, leading to a more severe emotional state or clinical depression.

Depression and all the negative feelings that can be associated with becoming an empty nester are not to be taken lightly. This can be a dangerous time and transition in the most extreme situations. At the very least, this time can be challenging and emotional for yourself and your child.

After completing this section, I need to add a disclaimer. This chapter is about the threats an Empty Nest parent may face. My goal is to summarize and share the threats an Empty Nest parent may face. This chapter is not about threat remediation; therefore, I have purposely not included solutions or support suggestions for depression. But due to the serious nature of this topic, I do want to say that if you or someone you know is experiencing symptoms of depression, it's vital to seek professional help.

D #2—Disownment

Disownment is the act of a child rejecting or renouncing their family or parental relationship. It looks threatening just to put these words on paper. I have repeatedly underscored the time, effort, and sacrifice a parent or parents make for their child. It seems excessive that a child would break away and disown their most significant support system in life, but it happens. I hate to break it to you, but it is happening more and more generationally. In his book *Fault Lines: Fractured Families and How to Mend Them*, Dr. Karl Pillemar, a professor of human development at Cornell University, stated that 27 percent of Americans, more than one in four, are estranged from their families. Of the 1,300 people Pillemer surveyed, 10 percent reported being estranged from a parent or child.

Raising a child is not a transactional relationship. The years of support you put into the relationship do not guarantee an ongoing successful relationship. As you transition into the complexity of an Empty Nest, your college-bound child is facing severe pressures of their own. The BestColleges.com 2022 College Student Mental Health Report, a survey made up of a thousand college students in the United States, found:

- Seventy-seven percent of college students experienced moderate to severe psychological distress.
- Thirty-five percent of students were diagnosed with anxiety.
- Twenty-seven percent had depression.

- In 2021, 28 percent of students said they often feel isolated from others.

Beyond struggling while away from home, college-student family relationships may not be as positive as one would believe. The American College Health Association published its fall 2021 survey comprising forty-one schools with 33,204 student participants. The students were asked questions about their mental and physical health. Two survey questions specifically underscore this point:

Within the last twelve months, have you had problems or challenges with any of the following? Family

1. No 65.5%
2. Yes 34.5%

To what extent did the following issue(s) cause you distress within the last twelve months? Family

1. No Distress 2.6%
2. Minimal Distress 30.6%
3. Moderate Distress 39.0%
4. High Distress 27.7%

This data shows that roughly one in three college students surveyed stated they had problems or challenges with their families. Further, two in three stated that they had moderate or high distress with their family. This data isn't good; it's alarming. Earlier in the book, I stated that I would use a child going off to college as my default example. However, one could imagine that, in the case of a child joining the military or venturing into the working world, it is highly likely that the pressures, anxiety, and emotions of these challenging scenarios would be equally valid, if not more significant, than the college students surveyed.

Why may a child cut off all ties and relationships with their parents? The reasons behind disownment vary widely and highly depend on individual and family circumstances. That aside, I summarized my research and have listed the five most common reasons children may cut ties with their parents:

- **Abuse**: Physical, emotional, verbal, or sexual abuse from a parent or family member. The scenario triggering disownment is that, once the child is out of the house, they can cease contact and protect themselves from further abuse.

- **Differences in beliefs or values**: A child with different religious beliefs, sexuality, or a value set that conflicts with their parents.

- **Interference in life decisions**: A situation where a child feels their parents are interfering with their life decisions, such as their choice of major, partner, or career path. This includes overly controlling or demanding actions by a parent.

- **Parental neglect**. Whether intentional or unintentional, parental neglect can lead to feelings of abandonment and emotional distress. An example would be a child who feels their parent(s) failed to provide for them emotionally, financially, or otherwise.

- **Betrayal / breach of trust**: A child may feel betrayed by their parent due to a breach of trust, such as a parent's infidelity, lying about an important matter, or sharing confidential information.

The Empty Nest transition is about risk. The changes in proximity, focus, and self-realization for a parent or child open up a window of both possibilities and threats. As I have repeatedly said, relationships come into question during this time. The child-parent relationship can be at risk. Due to your child no longer residing in your home and young adult immaturity, cutting ties becomes much more accessible. For the first time in your child's life, distance from you allows them to disengage with you.

> **For the first time in your child's life, distance from you allows them to disengage with you.**

A Year of Silence

In my junior year in college, I had a run-in with my father on Thanksgiving night. The conflict arose with a simple disagreement, but unlike any differences of our mutual past, this evening was the first time I pushed back and verbally fought with my father. This not-so-thankful Thanksgiving argument resulted in us not speaking to each other for over a year. It is safe to say we were both very stubborn, regardless of who was right or wrong.

The backstory of the argument isn't essential, but the context of the situation is. I was a young adult paying my way through college and providing for myself. I felt emancipated. My father, who had provided for me for eighteen years, was no longer in a controlling position. He was flexing his parent-child authority while I was flexing my adult-parent muscle. Power, control, letting go, and independence are the underlying themes of our conflict. We each saw the situation differently. I walked out of the house that night, intending not to return. Honestly, he was powerless to stop me. I think this was an "ah-ha" moment for him.

After a year of silence, we reconnected and lived a pleasant parent-adult life until his recent passing. I'm not proud of the Thanksgiving situation or my year of stubbornness, but looking back, it took this "breakup," for lack of a better term, to reset our relationship as adults. To this day, I believe this conflict needed to happen. At the same time, this is not a desirable approach, and separation from any of my children for a year would be horrible. And now that he is gone, I regret it even more. This is a threat.

Remember my "selling the helicopter" example? This was my way of relinquishing control over my children so that a big Thanksgiving breakup would never occur. My need to guide, marshal, and, yes, control certain aspects of their lives throughout high school had to change as they became adults. I had to change so they could grow and flex their independence. I had to change to ensure a year of silence didn't come back to haunt me with my children.

Disownment Is a Threat

You can control a baby, and you can discipline a teen, but you will have a hard time imposing your will on an adult child. Adults have the latitude and legal right to make their own choices. You are powerless to stop your child from disowning, cutting off contact, or initiating a year of silence with you. There may be consequences for their action, but they are in control. I wish the solution were as simple as, "Don't do any of those five things that make children disown their parents, and you'll be fine." However, relationships and individual emotions are more complex than that.

The five most common examples point to things a parent may have done or what a child perceives that a parent may have done to cause the disownment. This situation is not always the case. In my research, there were examples in which parents were not the catalyst or responsible for the ties being cut but the victims. The following three examples are the most common I came across in my research as to why a child could be the cause of the disownment:

- **Mental health issues**: This is particularly true in cases where a mental health issue brings about depression and anxiety. Examples of this would be bipolar disorder, borderline personality disorder, and substance use disorder. There were many in this category.
- **Outside influences**: This example involves a friend, family member, or romantic partner having emotional or undue influence on an adult child. This "outside" person encourages or instigates cutting ties with a parent or parents. Often, this is a romantic partner.
- **Narcissistic personality**: If your child has a narcissistic personality disorder, they have an inflated sense of self-importance, a lack of empathy, and a need for admiration. In this situation, an adult child may feel manipulated or exploited by their parent, regardless of whether they have been, and may choose to cut ties.

As unlikely as disownment or cutting ties may seem to the average single empty nester, the parent-child and parent-adult relationships are complex and evolving. There are aspects of yourself you can control moving forward, but there is also a history and outside influences you cannot change. For the child, this is a relationship they can now define as they leave the nest and become more independent. For parents, this threat is terrifying and real.

D #3-Disconnection

Disconnection is defined as becoming detached or withdrawn or being isolated and detached. One of the significant threats a single parent may face when their child leaves is disconnection. Practically, disconnection is when one withdraws from others, intentionally or unintentionally, and isolates themselves from life.

To fully understand the threat of disconnection for a single parent, we can divide it into three distinct subgroups: emotional, social, and practical disconnection.

Emotional Disconnection

The definition of Empty Nest Syndrome is essentially the same as emotional disconnection. This includes one's loss of identity, triggered when parenting is a central part of a single parent's identity. The Empty Nest can leave one feeling lost and unsure of who they are without their child. This can lead to withdrawal and isolation. Similarly, grief and loneliness are two strong emotions. Single parents may experience different stages of grief as they adjust to the absence of their child. Like loss of identity, this can lead to social withdrawal and disconnection from others. Finally, going through any life stage transition without a support network can be difficult. Single parents without a partner may have a smaller support network than couples. Without a support network in place, a single parent may find it harder to share their struggles and cope with emotional challenges, leading to increased isolation.

Some emotional disconnection is typical among all transitioning empty nesters, whether single or married, with varying degrees of seriousness.

Social Disconnection

Social disconnection happens when the routine of friendships and social encounters changes significantly due to a child leaving the nest. For a single parent, the finality or end of a parent's child-based social circles can dramatically affect their social activity. Adult friendships are often gained through a child's activities (sports, clubs, interests). Since these interactions usually revolve around children, many single parents have stated they have fewer social connections or opportunities to connect when their child's activities cease (once their child leaves).

Another cited social disconnection is a single parent's hesitation to date. The top cited reasons why a single parent may be disinclined to engage with a romantic partner are fear of judgment and difficulty finding compatible partners. This attitude can keep single parents from building new relationships, thus leading to social isolation. Lack of financial stability or a single parent feeling that they don't have enough money to interact in social situations (dinners, dates, bars, events) can preclude them from venturing out and interacting socially.

Finally, being surrounded by unfavorable social comparisons, such as seeing seemingly happy couples or other peers navigate the Empty Nest transition, can trigger feelings of loneliness and isolation in single parents.

Practical Disconnection

There are many practical examples of disconnection. Everything from transitioning to having an empty house to adjusting to the lack of physical touch are realities of living alone. Compounding these feelings of isolation, a single parent may experience a loss of structure and adherence to daily habits. Long-established parent-based routines such as sleep patterns, eating habits, and physical movement can change when a child's dependency ceases. These changes can negatively affect one's outlook, mood, and energy levels. Many single parents state that their workload increases once their child leaves. Balancing work, home maintenance, and emotional needs without the help of a child can leave single parents exhausted and again with less time for social interaction. An increase in the ability to work from home also limits social interaction. The final practical disconnection revolves around a single parent's reliance on technology. Although this is an issue with people of all ages, many single parents stated that they increased their phone use as a way to cope with loneliness and stay connected. In some circumstances, this increase can lead to excessive social media use or online interactions, leading to not only a dependency on social platforms but compounding feelings of isolation and disconnection from real-world relationships.

The three forms of disconnection can negatively impact mental and physical health, increasing the risk of depression, anxiety, and other health problems. Not focusing on building and maintaining strong social connections may diminish one's emotional support structure and personal well-being. If single parents don't work to rediscover their identity and purpose, engaging in non-child-related activities, hobbies, and social outlets, they can fall further into seclusion.

Although not all single parents experience disconnection, and some thrive during the Empty Nest phase, it is a threat. Recognizing the signs of disconnection is essential to proactively preparing for a smoother transition.

Before closing out the topic of Empty Nest Threats, we must dive into the most significant threat: the fourth D, deprioritization. Depression is bad, disownment is sad, and disconnection leads to a life alone. These three threats are some of the least desired outcomes a parent can face. However, deprioritization is slightly different from all others. It can be a passive and silent killer. By unconsciously or consciously not focusing on yourself, you are potentially sabotaging your relationships and life. Deprioritization brings about the potential to invite unintended threats into your life.

Let's explore this silent threat together.

CHAPTER 10 KEY POINTS

- An Empty Nest transition can trigger the start and realization of any Empty Nest Threat.

- The four Ds of Empty Nest Threats are depression, disownment, disconnection, and deprioritization.

- Depression and disownment are on the rise in the United States for both parents and their children.

- There are three forms of disconnection: emotional, social, and practical. Each leads to detachment and isolation.

"The only person you are destined to become is the person you decide to be."

—RALPH WALDO EMERSON

CHAPTER ELEVEN

Empty Nest Threat #4— Deprioritization

Your Priorities

BEFORE WE DISCUSS deprioritization as an Empty Nest threat, let's discuss your priorities. For many parents today, raising a child is an all-consuming task. When not actively raising a child, the second most prominent time commitment and priority a single parent faces is likely working full-time.

Most parents spend excessive time ensuring their family has access to the things they want in life for themselves and their children. To this end, most single parents have inevitably made many personal sacrifices and negotiated trade-offs for their children. Single parents have given up the majority of their free time willingly and shelved the pursuit of individual goals, friendships, intimate relationships, and interests so that they can give themselves freely and intentionally to their children. This is incredibly admirable for single parents who have made these trade-offs and sacrifices without the aid of an ex-spouse.

Let's shift a bit and focus on you. I will assume that you have done the following things over the years. First, you have made your parenting responsibilities for your child the number-one priority. Following that, you have prioritized yourself, your greater family unit, and perhaps your job in second, third, or fourth. Since we are all different people living different lives, we can assume that each of us has our own ranking with the list of roles mentioned. Let's do a quick exercise to see where your priorities are.

Exercise 1–Your Priorities

Directions: In the following table, rank what has been your top priority (time-consuming and effort-consuming on your part) to the least priority since the birth of your first child. There are six priorities, so read each and rank them from one priority to six (last priority).

Start: Take a quick moment to reflect on your priorities since the birth of your first child. Then, start ranking.

PRIORITY	YOUR RANK
Yourself	
Children	
Friends	
Parents	
Family	
Job	

How did you do? Were you surprised at your ranking? What was number six? This exercise is harder than it looks. Let's go one step further.

Exercise 2–Your Believed Child's Priorities

Directions: In the following table, mentally or physically rank what you believe is your teenage or young adult child/children's top priority (time-consuming and effort on their part) to the least priority. There are seven priorities in this exercise. Read each and rank them from one to seven (last priority).

Start: Take a quick moment right now to reflect on what you believe your child's priorities are Now rank for your child.

PRIORITY	DESCRIPTION	YOUR BELIEVED CHILD'S RANK
Themselves	Their Self-Care / Needs	
You / The Parent	Communicating	
School	Homework / Attendance	
Activities	Sports / Clubs / Interests	
Family	Siblings / Household	
Friends	Relationships	
Job	Money	

Here are my results for both rankings. I found this exercise equally difficult for my child as for me.

MY RANKING	MY BELIEVED CHILD'S RANK
#1 Family	#1 School
#2 Job	#2 Activities
#3 Child (Children)	#3 Themselves
#4 Friends	#4 Friends
#5 Myself	#5 Family
#6 Parents	#6 Parents (you)
	#7 Job

There is no judgment in your ranking or your rankings for your children. We all make priority choices and trade-offs daily. When it comes to parenting, given the work and effort it takes to raise a child in today's world, I'm willing to bet that you prioritized a child or family first. Perhaps due to the cost and financial pressures of living and raising a child today, you may have prioritized your job/work highly. Although we will go into this later, I prioritized family first and then my job before my children. It doesn't mean I loved my job more than I loved my children, but financial pressures prioritized finances (a job) over my children. I missed school plays, sports events, and other things for work, essentially money. Again, there should be no judgment in my or your priority ranking. Something has to come first, just as something has to be last.

If children or family were on the top of your list, your priority as a parent is supported by data. According to the Pew Research Center's 2022 Survey of US Parents, 30 percent of parents state that parenting is their *most important job*, while an additional 57 percent say it is one of their most important. When asked about the *most important aspect of who you are*, 35 percent of moms surveyed said being a mother, while 24 percent of dads said being a father. The priority exercise and data demonstrate a realistic view of parenting and surviving in today's society and how we are forced to make choices—prioritization and deprioritization of responsibilities and roles are problems all parents face. Raising children, balancing a career, keeping the family unit together, and looking after your needs and those of others are herculean tasks for anyone, let alone a single parent. There is only so much time to complete all your responsibilities, and you only have so many hours in the day and the energy to succeed in each role. Our choices have consequences, and negative consequences can become Empty Nest Threats.

> ### Prioritization and deprioritization of responsibilities and roles are problems all parents face.

Here is the sneaky catch to prioritization and becoming an empty nester. The prioritization balancing acts you have grown accustomed to while raising your child change. For example, two of my top three (children and family) will no longer be daily active top priorities once my last child leaves the nest. As a single empty nester, your priority ranking will inevitably shift, and this shift, like any significant life change, will trigger introspection, forcing you to reflect on your purpose, your feelings, and future actions.

Becoming a single empty nester doesn't stop at introspection. You will physically and emotionally find yourself back in a household of one. This will be a new lifestyle situation for you, which you likely haven't experienced in decades since before you had children. You will have more time to refocus and reflect on your relationships, physical and mental state, and life. Big questions such as, "What will I do during this next phase of my life," and "What do I want moving forward?" are just two of the inevitable questions that will potentially come forward. You won't be the only one reflecting; your child may also be reflecting on their new independent life as an adult. The reflections may differ, but this time is a significant physical and mental life shift for both of you.

As with any self-reflection concerning your life, inevitably, there will be positive and negative thoughts.

For example:

- How do I feel about my life at this point?
- How do I feel about my physical and mental health?
- How is my relationship with my child?
- Does my child want to interact with me / still need me?
- What do I want to focus my time on now?

- Do I have the support group of friends and family I want?
- Do I want to explore romantic relationships?
- What's next?

Any answer or outcome to these questions is possible, especially when considering that they aren't simple yes or no answers but accurately measured in degrees. Suppose the answer to any of these questions was negative, meaning you had concerns about your feelings, relationships, or outlook. In that case, you may face three Empty Nest Threats: depression, disownment, or disconnection.

> **"Even if you follow other people's advice and model successful people and their blueprints, you will still fail if you don't have confidence in yourself. Everything – absolutely everything – starts with you."**
>
> **—PAULO COELHO**

My Deprioritization

The company I worked for was acquired when I was thirty-five years old. This was a situation where I was given six months' salary. Fortunately, the job market was good then, and I was confident my family's financial situation would be fine. I decided to give myself three to five months to not work and do everything I always wished I had time for in the past. Working sixty hours a week with a family, I didn't have time for my pursuits. Or so I told myself. This was my chance. I remember discussing my plan with a friend, Ken, a month before my last day. I was espousing all of the activities on my "free time" list. I vividly remember Ken saying, "It will be interesting to see what you do with that time." I dismissed his comment, not caring to respond to it, and I felt a tad insulted he even made the statement. Why would Ken question what I said I was going to do? My list had the following things: lose weight and exercise, spend more time with my three children, learn the guitar, write, and complete a hodgepodge of housekeeping tasks. Maybe it wasn't easy, but it was doable. Guess what? Over the five months of not working, did I exercise? No. Did I lose weight? No. Did I learn the guitar or write anything? No. I'm embarrassed to admit it, but I completed the easy one-off tasks and spent a little more time with my children, walking them to school and volunteering in their class (not the norm). But most of all, I surfed the internet for five months and squandered most of that time. For years, I told myself, "If I had the time to do things, I would do them." I had the time, but I didn't. Ken's insinuation was correct.

This story is meaningful because it points out several things about human nature and me. First, I believed my own narrative about why I wasn't doing these things, which was a lie. Second, even when given time, eight to ten hours a day five days a week, I still didn't focus on what I wanted. It wasn't that I didn't have ambitious goals or desire to do these things; I did. And it wasn't that I didn't have time. Again, I had a lot of time. The core of my issue was that I deprioritized myself, my goals, and the gift of time by treating these as unimportant. I don't think I ignored my goals consciously; I didn't do them.

Deprioritization is treating something as the lowest importance. If that something is you, it can manifest into the most severe Empty Nest Threat.

We have dipped our toes into priorities and what deprioritization looks like; now, let's discover how deprioritization occurs, how it can sneak into decades of routine, and how it silently settles in. It's as serious as each of the other three Ds but much more dangerous in that it can make the other three happen. Deprioritization can lead to depression, and it can cause a relationship to fail (disownment), and it can drive disconnection. Unfortunately, many of us may not be aware that deprioritization will happen or is currently happening.

Active Individual versus Active Parent

I have always felt a natural tension between being an active individual and an active parent. All parents with children take on both of these roles. As an active parent, you cannot set this role aside. You cannot stop feeding your child, ignore their need for attention, or put off their schedule. Child-rearing is a full-time job and commitment because a human child cannot fend for themselves. This is true with an infant when we reflect on the late-night feedings and lack of sleep. This continues with toddlers, who need to be on constant watch while they explore and taste everything around them. A primary school-age child looks to a parent for life structure, including care, meals, school, and social activities. Pre-teen and young adults need structure and guidance from a balanced hand to deal with drama, dilemmas, and their navigation into adulthood. I'm exhausted just reflecting on it.

Let's contrast an active parent with an active individual. Being an active individual is also a full-time commitment. However, unlike being an active child-parent, you can put your wants and needs on the back burner. You can, for lack of a better term, "take advantage of yourself" and ignore your physical and emotional health if faced with time constraints, pressure, or exhaustion. You can make this trade-off of time and attention for yourself, knowing that this is an impossibility for a child. This simple distinction indicates that the parent-child relationship is sometimes more focus-driven and demanding than the individual one. The case for a single parent needing to be present, active, and involved in their child's life doesn't need to be made. It is a reality of parenting. One can make the same case for needing to be present, active, and involved in their own life. The problem is parents tend to deprioritize themselves.

A Parent's Love versus Self-Love

Let me share a simple example that underscores the emotional difference between the parent-child relationship and the relationship with oneself.

Let's think about the love you have for your child. At what point did you love your child deeply? I have asked many parents this question, and the number-one answer is, "At the moment of birth when they first held their child in their arms." This happened to me three times. Once you see your baby's face for the first time, the deep love and bond are instantaneous. Remarkably, we can love something instantly and deeply. On the science side, evidence suggests that this connection is biological. In a Stanford Children's Health article titled "Give 'Em Some Skin," Dr. Susan Crowe, a clinical associate professor of obstetrics and gynecology at Stanford School of Medicine, states, "After the umbilical cord is cut, the baby should be moved up to the mother's chest. The skin-to-skin contact causes a release in oxytocin—known as the 'love hormone'—in the mom." Certainly, some parents loved their child when they or their partner became pregnant, while others may have taken longer to develop a deeply connected love for their offspring. Regardless of when this happens, we can agree that this "instantaneous love" from a parent to a child is an evolutionary requirement for the continuation of the species.

Let's briefly discuss self-love, as we will dive deeper into this topic in chapter 14. Self-love means having a high regard for your own well-being and happiness. Self-love means caring for your needs and not sacrificing your well-being to please others. From that definition alone, you can see where this is going. Perhaps surprisingly, one in three people globally struggle with self-acceptance and self-value. In a survey by Vitagene, a former DNA testing company, 65 percent of respondents acknowledge that they need greater self-love. Additionally, 44 percent of respondents said self-love was a crucial component of their mental wellness. Unfortunately, only 13 percent of women claim they routinely practice self-love, and even more dismally, only 5 percent of males practice self-love. Although we'd like to believe we prioritize our well-being and happiness through self-love, the data proves otherwise. The purpose of this example is not to one-up a parent-child relationship over an individual's self-care or make you feel bad about your prioritizations or deprioritizations in the past but rather to demonstrate that these two types of love develop differently in a different time frame, and are not the same.

Upon reflection, you have likely done a very natural and common thing. You chose to prioritize your parent-child relationship out of necessity and had to deprioritize yourself while raising a child. This isn't to say you treated yourself poorly or lived with self-doubt, but perhaps there were many situations where your priority, attention, and focus on your children came at the expense of your happiness and health. For some of us, it's possible that the child focus became more of a routine and a habit rather than a conscious choice. As we all know, habits are hard to break, and routines are easy to fall into and repeat. This is a prime example of deprioritization.

Your Parental Life Cycle

To further identify deprioritization, let's look at your parental life cycle. With the addition of your first child, whether you were married or not at the time, your life as an individual or couple shifted. Although this is a miraculous time for any parent, it is expected that your time, effort, and attention will now focus on the family or the child. Your priorities changed to child-rearing priorities. Throughout this time, your division of labor tended to fall into routine. Feeding, cleaning, reading, comforting, and raising a child are organized by routine. Routines shouldn't be considered wrong; they help manage your household and life.

As your life cycle of a child-focused routine continues, you are also keeping your life's organizational and financial aspects on track. Throughout this period, your routines repeat themselves (daily, monthly, annually), and you are forced to spend less time on yourself due to the focus on family. This deprioritization of oneself doesn't happen intentionally; it just happens. Let's face it: as part of a parent's day-to-day life cycle, you must balance your time and effort with a child or children, not to mention a job, a household, extended family, and friends. With all these competing priorities, it is easy to see how you deprioritized yourself.

The prior example underscores how single parents can't put off child-rearing. However, the same holds true for the other aspects of a single parent's life. One has to show up for work, meet deadlines, pay bills, and buy food. All of these actions have dire consequences if they are not done. Individually, deprioritizing oneself is the easy choice, and one's needs can be deprioritized in the moment without immediate severe implications. Because of this, the threat gets bigger.

Fast forward three years, seven years, or eighteen years, and you continue to move forward in your routine. You have been an active and admirable participative parent. Throughout this life cycle, you have ensured every aspect of the home and home upkeep, friend and family relationships, finances and career, and outside relationships have all been taken care of to the best of your abilities. All parents make these choices to meet their obligations and keep their lives moving forward. However, deprioritization can quickly settle in, become the norm, and be unintentionally present.

Deprioritization of oneself can present itself in many ways. You may have routinely spent less time and energy on keeping yourself physically healthy. You may have set aside maintaining existing and developing new friendships. You may have spent less effort reducing your anxiety, relaxing, or keeping your mental health a priority. You may have deferred opportunities to pursue romantic relationships. You may have put travel, adventure, and fun on the back burner. Unfortunately, there is an endless list of things you may have deprioritized. The worst-case scenario is that you routinely, possibly for decades, didn't invest time and energy on your own needs. A parenting life without focusing on yourself is the quintessential example of deprioritization.

At this point, you may be experiencing one or several of these reactions or emotions:

- You are saddened or disenchanted by the realization that you have deprioritized yourself.
- You are slightly angry or defensive because you had to make these trade-offs.
- You are committed and confident that you found and have stuck to a good balance between parenting and your needs.

I came off a little defensive about my deprioritization. I hope that you have found a good balance. Unfortunately, and you know what I'm going to tell you, the data states that single parents are more likely to have deprioritized themselves for the sake of parenting and other responsibilities. Before we wrap up this chapter, let's complete a final exercise to give us a clear picture of our individualized deprioritization threat. We already looked at our high-level priority ranking in exercise 1. Now let's look at what specific things we may have deprioritized.

Exercise 3 – Your Deprioritization

Directions: In the following table, mentally or physically check, circle, or cross off the actions or activities you have personally deprioritized in the last eighteen months. Feel free to extend or compact the eighteen-month timeline to get a bigger or more focused picture. The goal is to get a snapshot of you during a recent timeframe.

Start: Take a quick moment to review and reflect on the following twenty-eight actions or activities. Which have you deprioritized over the last eighteen months (or on your custom timeline)?

PHYSICAL HEALTH	TIME WITH FRIENDS	ROMANTIC RELATIONSHIPS / DATING	FITNESS / EXERCISE
Time with extended family	Pursuing hobbies and interests	Mental health	Sleep
Career advancement	Travel and vacations	Eating healthy	Social activities and outings
Self-care routines and pampering	Professional development	Household chores/ organization	Financial investment/retirement
Educational pursuits / academic goals	Personal time for relaxation	Non-child based volunteer work	Personal purchases or luxuries
Personal goals/aspirations	Non-child based community involvement	Home improvement/ projects or renovation	Reading / arts and crafts
Attending social events	Annual checkups (dentist, doctor, etc.)	Paying off debt/ emergency fund	Personal appearance (haircuts, clothes, style)

How did you do? What is your number out of the twenty-eight? Are you surprised by your number? There is no correct number, as some single parents may deprioritize only a few items from the list while others may find themselves deprioritizing many. Your number versus anyone else will vary greatly depending on individual circumstances. Additionally, some actions or activities may fall into the category of something you wouldn't do if you had all the time and money in the world. You now have a number or a list of actions and activities you have deprioritized. So why is this important? Why is this a significant threat? Let's find the answer to those questions.

Why Is This Important?

Understanding your deprioritization is essential because there are some significant potential negative consequences if you consistently deprioritize many things on the list. Here are a few of the more serious negative outcomes.

Your Physical and Mental Health:

- **Increased risk of chronic health issues:** Poor sleep habits, lack of exercise, healthy eating, and preventive care can lead to obesity, diabetes, heart disease, and other health problems.
- **Increased risk of mental health issues:** Neglecting stress management, self-care, and professional help or

support when needed, such as therapy, can lead to anxiety, depression, and burnout.

Your Social and Emotional Well-Being:

- **Isolation and loneliness:** Neglecting social connections and relationships can lead to feelings of isolation and loneliness, negatively impacting mental and physical health.
- **Strained relationships with family and friends:** Lack of time and energy for relationships can lead to misunderstandings, resentment, and decreased personal support.
- **Difficulty forming new relationships:** Neglecting dating or social activities can make it harder to meet new people and build romantic or platonic relationships.

Financial Instability:

- **Increased debt:** Putting off debt repayment or neglecting financial planning can lead to increased financial stress and hardship in the future.
- **Lack of emergency savings:** Not having an emergency fund can leave you vulnerable to financial shocks and disruptions.
- **Difficulty affording retirement:** Neglecting retirement savings can lead to financial insecurity and dependence on others in your later years.

Personal Stagnation and Regret:

- **Unfulfilled dreams and aspirations:** Putting your own goals and interests on hold can lead to feelings of missed opportunities and regret later in life.
- **Loss of identity and purpose:** Neglecting personal development and interests can make it harder to maintain a sense of identity and purpose outside your parenting role.
- **Reduced sense of accomplishment and satisfaction:** Focusing solely on others' needs can leave you feeling drained and lacking a sense of personal fulfillment.

These are the potential worst-case scenarios; not everyone who deprioritizes any of the twenty-eight actions and activities will experience these negative outcomes. But if one of these negative consequences is true for you, let alone several, we must acknowledge that we have been and are living with a real deprioritization threat.

Put an End to the Threats

Your Empty Nest transition doesn't have to be full of threats. It doesn't have to contain any of the four Ds. There is a quote by the Thoughtful Beast: "I do not need to find happiness. I can create happiness all on my own." This quote is spot on. Today, you can prepare for your Empty Nest journey and avoid or minimize your vulnerability to the four Ds. There don't have to be these significant threats in your future.

The first step toward helping yourself is something you just did. You now understand the situation, potential impact, and reality of Empty Nest Threats. By exploring this topic, you have already made a giant leap in correcting a potential negative Empty Nest outcome. Additionally, you are personally aware and can now be more empathetic of the challenges a friend, child, or family member may face during their Empty Nest transition.

As we close this chapter, I am reminded of an "ah-ha" moment when I started working through and planning my Empty Nest journey. After my son graduated high school, we had everything dialed in before he left for college. His dorm room and roommate were set. He had a new college bike for transportation. He had a good food plan, expenses covered, and tuition lined up and ready to go. I realized as he was being set up to live his "best life" off to college, it was up to me alone to start focusing and creating my own "best life" back at home. I still had two more children in the pre-launch high school phase, but perhaps it was time to up my prioritization while still meeting the demands of my family. This became my focus.

Over the following two chapters, we will define the Empty Nest Opportunit, which will lead you to develop your Empty Nest Blueprint. Armed with a blueprint, you can be the positive force you want to be for this next stage of your life. I created my best Empty Nest life by seizing Empty Nest

Opportunities, building a blueprint, and following the plans we will discuss. Let's get started building yours.

CHAPTER 11 KEY POINTS

- The fourth and final D of the Empty Nest Threats is deprioritization.

- Deprioritization is when you treat something (in this case, your wants and needs) as being of the lowest importance.

- We each make choices and deprioritize; the degree of deprioritization matters.

- The worst-case scenarios of deprioritization are serious, frightening, and potentially life-threatening.

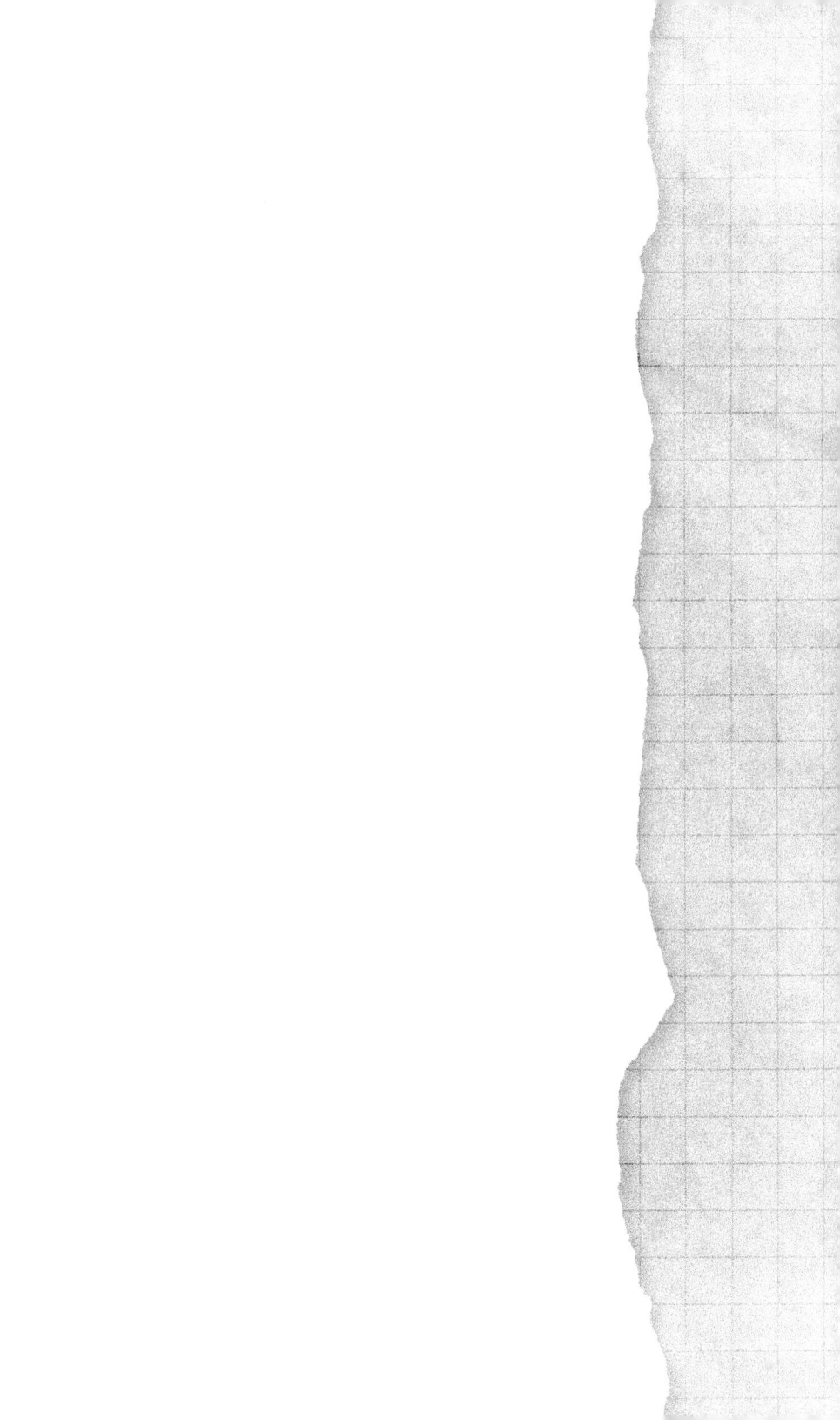

"Being a single parent is so much harder, but more rewarding, than I ever expected."

CHAPTER TWELVE

Empty Nest Opportunities

IT IS A GIVEN that your life will change when your children leave the house. This change will impact you and your child, but it doesn't have to be the worst-case scenario foretold in the Empty Nest Threats. You aren't destined to experience the four Ds: depression, disownment, disconnection, and deprioritization. The transition into becoming an empty nester can be one of the best periods of your life. The Empty Nest Opportunities are about setting yourself up for a fantastic future.

This chapter focuses on shifting your mindset and routine and starting a life plan you can be excited about. Over the following few chapters, you will be asked to reflect and write answers to questions, create lists, and put pen to paper. If, thus far, you have only chosen to think through the questions and lists you have been prompted for, that's okay; however, moving forward, you will want to write down answers and experiences so that the result will be more impactful and helpful when you create your plans. Whether you take notes on your phone, a computer, or a pad of paper, I suggest getting prepared to write.

You will discover how to genuinely shift toward your best Empty Nest life. After reading this chapter and completing the four exercises, you will have the mindset to build your blueprint and make your Empty Nest Opportunities a reality. Let's get started.

You, at the Center

This chapter, in fact, this book, is focused on you. You are learning, discovering, and building your blueprint. All the examples, statistics, and words were put on paper to help you develop your best Empty Nest future. With this realization, we need to focus on you before we go any further. There is a quote by Kelly Rudolph, "Taking care of yourself makes you stronger for everyone in your life... including you." The Empty Nest Opportunity you have is solely in your power.

Nowhere in this book is your child, friends, or family asked to do anything. It's all about you.

Your relationships, the joy you create in your life, and your Empty Nest Blueprint can only happen if you are in the right mindset with yourself. The following two exercises are focused on you. Take as much time as you need to complete them—the longer, the better—but minimally, it will take three to five minutes. Let's discover how amazing you are.

Exercise 1—Your Qualities and Characteristics

Directions: I'd like you to write down your positive qualities and characteristics. Consider your strengths, skills, talents, accomplishments, and the positive impact you have had on others. You have many examples of each of these things in your head. Read the definition and write as many answers as you can. Try for a minimum of five in each category.

POSITIVE QUALITIES AND CHARACTERISTICS
Strengths – What you are good at doing
Skills – What you can do
Talents – Your innate ability or natural aptitude
Accomplishments – Your achievements through effort
Positive Impact – Your beneficial influence on others/things

Start: Ready? Try not to get caught up in the definitions or differences. Just start writing.

How'd you do? Are you a loyal friend? Can you yo-yo well? Are you good at painting, remembering movie facts, or driving? Did you flash through your past and see the participation ribbon you received in third grade, or did you remember loaning money to a family member? If you just thought of several more, write them down. By the way, good job putting pen to paper. I'm sure you are an amazing person who now possesses a physical list full of positive qualities and characteristics about yourself. There is one more step in this exercise.

Review your list and choose the top three to five qualities you feel are most important and meaningful to you.

Do you have your three to five? Because we are doing this together, my five top qualities were a sense of humor, generosity, the ability to see different perspectives, willpower, and empathy. The three to five things you chose are the traits you value, appreciate, and like about yourself. There is also a school of thought that they are traits you value in others, but we won't go down that philosophical hole. All the qualities and characteristics on your list represent only a small fraction of your greatness. If we asked everyone you know to come up with five more qualities and characteristics, you would have a binder full of the impact you have had on others' lives and descriptions of what's great about you. I think we did it. I think we discovered what an amazing person you are.

Since we have just joined "Team Positive," let's quickly do one more exercise—and this one is easy. As we are all aware, we are often our own worst critics. Right now, let's decide to be our own best champions. Let's treat ourselves with the same kindness we offer others when we compliment them.

Exercise 2 – Three Compliments

Directions: Write down three compliments you want, need, and should hear from yourself daily. Just so it is impactful, let's say you must tell yourself these three compliments daily for the rest of your life. Make them count because you may be hearing them for at least thirty more years.

Start: How did you do? Was it harder than you thought? I found this exercise to be difficult. Not because three compliments were hard to think of but because creating three compliments for the rest of my life put more pressure on the assignment. What did you find out? Are you likable, fashion-conscious, a good singer, generous, powerful? Complimenting someone makes them feel appreciated, good, and positive, underscoring their self-worth while building their confidence. A compliment is a gift we give to others. Why don't we give this gift to ourselves more often? Your three compliments are yours to keep. Repeat at will and add to them. Don't you deserve to feel this gift every day? We all do.

In the next section, I will ask the person you just recognized and complimented to commit, embrace, and pursue their Empty Nest future. Out of all the things we do throughout our days, an individual rarely reflects on the totality of their life. Much of our waking lives are focused on the moment. And the times when we reflect on the past can often be a singular fond memory or, worse yet, some guilt, regret, or experience that may not have gone well. We are amazingly good at cherry-picking instances, both good and bad, in our past, but we aren't so good about panning out and seeing our lives as a whole. In the last two exercises, you rediscovered all the positive strengths and talents you possess and their impact on others. And we admittedly know there are even more. Moving forward, we will channel all that's great in you to build your Empty Nest Blueprint. Even more remarkable is that by the time you finish this book, you will have increased your accomplishments and positively impacted some of the most important relationships in your life. Remember, you are at the center.

Your Life

On becoming an empty nester, your life thus far has consisted of three phases: your childhood, your pre-parent phase, and your parent phase. Each phase has been full of self-discovery, learning, life struggles, and rich experiences. If we look at your life as a written history, your childhood and pre-parent phase could be considered volumes one and two. To that end, your single parenting life story would be a massive volume three. Like most parents, volume three would be filled with great experiences and memories such as birthdays, your child's and your accomplishments, and numerous times of laughter and love. And then there would be chapters filled with the challenges, unexpected issues, and hardships you as an individual and a single parent have faced along the way. All of the personal and shared experiences you have had add more and more depth to the books in volume three.

Upon completion of the active parenting phase, you would have your unique parenting story. The manuscript would be filled with anecdotes, knowledge, and emotions. It would be a printed representation of the life you have built. It would be an amazing read. A quote by Ariadna Thalía nicely fits here: "Everybody has their own story; everybody has their journey." Your life as a parent is one of the most significant commitments a person can make. And if you believe you only get one lifetime, the enormity of this fact is even more impactful.

Let's do some more work and set the stage to understand your Empty Nest Opportunity truly.

Exercise 3 - You

Directions: In this exercise, I will ask you to think about your life and engage in quick gratitude introspection. First, close your eyes and visualize the people, things, and experiences that have made up your life. As you visualize each thing, take a split second to be thankful for each picture that comes into your mind. Give yourself time to view whatever comes to mind, and then open your eyes when you feel done.

Start: How did you do? Hopefully, you visualized all the good you have in your life. Most importantly, hopefully, you realize you have much to be grateful for. When I do this gratitude exercise, my visualization usually starts with my immediate family, extended family, and friends. The list changes at times, but it generally consists of the following: family, friends, shelter, health, food, water, possessions, nature, and the planet. I can be grateful for the film *Pulp Fiction* or for the fact that I never have to eat an artichoke again in my lifetime.

Here is an extreme example: if we were to ask a prisoner in a cell serving a life sentence to complete this exercise, they could quickly close their eyes and be thankful for their health, books, sunshine, meals, shelter, and their ability to think and live. Even our prisoner has an endless number of things for which they could be thankful. There are so many random things each of us can be grateful for; no two gratitude moments are the same. This exercise is about perspective, the perspective that, no matter how difficult, you have endless things to be grateful for throughout your life.

Now, let's do the same exercise again, but only think of your child this time.

Exercise 4 – Your Child

Directions: Think about your child and engage in quick gratitude introspection. Think about them physically. Think about their positive qualities and character traits. Think about what you love about them, what makes them smile, and what about them makes you smile. Think about the shared experiences you have had together.

Remember, as you visualize each thing, take a split second to be thankful for each picture that comes into your mind. Open your eyes when you feel done.

Start. If you completed the exercise, the brief movie you just played in your head is a great gift. Everything you visualized builds the case for why you became a parent. The exercise you just completed was full of your parental experience, and yet there are still endless moments and memories you didn't think of or have long forgotten. The gift you just gave yourself is much bigger than your capacity to remember. Every moment, all of it, your entire parenting life, is what you have to be genuinely thankful for.

This section aims to give you a long-term perspective of what has been great about your life. I also want to remind you of your incredible life as an individual and a parent and all you have to be grateful for. Your history, the love you have experienced, and your life shared with others are best remembered and embraced using a long-term perspective.

Commit, Embrace, Pursue

You have been lucky enough to experience the last three phases of your life up until now. You have quickly reflected on your life. You created a visual movie of your life and child containing numerous things for which you are thankful. Hold on to the joy of those thoughts for one more moment, and then let them go. It's time to shift.

Right now, we are in the present time. And right now, you have some decisions to make. If you don't want the Empty Nest Ds (depression, disownment, disconnection, and deprioritization), then your goal is to embrace the Empty Nest Opportunities. Here are three things you need to decide, preferably right now, to make your opportunity a reality:

1. Commit to the Empty Nest stage of your life.

You have been a child, an adult, and a parent. You are entering the fourth phase of your life, the Empty Nest phase. This is your time and your opportunity to truly focus on you. Commit to dedicating yourself to your needs, wants, and dreams. Decide who you want to be, what you want to focus on, and who you can become during the remainder of your life. We will talk about the "how" later, but right now, decide that you want to commit yourself to this next stage in life. If you have made this commitment, you should be excited because you have decided to add endless more qualities and experiences to be grateful for from this point forward. Congratulations!

2. Embrace your power to change and fuel your desire to change.

With the prior commitment, you will have to change. The fact is, your living situation, companionship with your child, routine, and life are changing with this transition to empty nesting. This can be a tremendous burden you put on your shoulders or an opportunity to embrace your power to change. Choose to embrace change! Commit to changing what you prioritize, how you treat and think about yourself, how you view your future, and how you react to the world around you. This is not a request to be someone different, lose fifteen pounds, or pretend to be something you are not. Instead, this is your commitment to showing more self-love, support, and appreciation for yourself moving forward. We will cover the "what" and the "how" later in this book. But right now, you are deciding to focus on yourself and committing to embrace change for the better.

3. Pursue the best life you can imagine with your happiness in mind.

This pursuit translates to imagining your Empty Nest future, where your life is filled with excitement and fun. This doesn't mean hardships or struggles magically disappear; this commitment is about what you want to focus on in a "you-first" future. You are focusing on personal fulfillment, excitement, and fun. The happiness you generate for yourself becomes your top priority.

Seizing your Empty Nest Opportunities starts with these three decisions. Committing, embracing, and pursuing your best Empty Nest life would be best. Each decision is an internal commitment you make to yourself and a mindset you adopt moving forward. The ideal summary answer is:

- *I am entering a new phase in life.*
- *I am ready to prioritize myself.*
- *I want to create my best future.*

If you are genuinely ready to make these three commitments to yourself, then your "you-first" Empty Nest future has started and is well within reach.

Beyond making these three decisions, the next section is pivotal to your Empty Nest Opportunities. In it, you will discover how to leverage your advantage to create your best Empty Nest life.

The Empty Nest Advantage

The Empty Nest Threats chapter describes the issues many single parents face once their children depart. For most, the four Ds aren't intentional outcomes but situations that arise through a survival routine where all the pressures and responsibilities of life make one lose track of oneself. Looking back, it doesn't matter if you sacrificed for your child or neglected yourself or your dreams. There is no shame or blame as to where you are today. Being a single parent is difficult. Since you can't change anything that has happened in the past, the three decisions you made in the last section will become the foundation of your future. You decided to commit, embrace, and pursue your best Empty Nest life. Therefore, your desire to change will enable you to leverage the Empty Nest Advantage to achieve your goals. This is your opportunity and the most significant thing you can do to guarantee the best Empty Nest future.

Your Empty Nest Advantage is the catalyst for achieving your Empty Nest Opportunities. That advantage is time. Throughout this book, the topic of time, more specifically, the dedicated time you have spent as a single parent and the time you will have as an empty nester, has come up repeatedly. To avoid repartition, let's summarize these two points in two sentences: "For the last two decades, you have spent an inordinate amount of time, daily, year after year, from diapers to diplomas, focusing on, caring for, and marshaling your child through life.

When active parenting stops and your child departs the home, the biggest change you will experience is more free time." There is nothing magical or even insightful about these statements; they are facts. In the research, in almost every article, and in my own survey of single empty nesters, having more time is the universal truth. Although this is an advantage for all empty nesters, it seems to be an even bigger advantage for single empty nesters since the time demands of a spouse aren't present.

You'll recall my story in chapter 11, where I had a six-month severance and decided to take time off and pursue whatever interests I wanted. Embarrassingly, you'll also recall that I semi-squandered it. I was given the gift of time, but I deprioritized myself and my ambitions. Essentially, the fourth D took hold. We can waste, squander, put off, and deprioritize time. Time is just an object, an opportunity that we can use to our advantage or not. You, however, won't suffer the same fate as I did in my five-month trial run because you have made the conscious decision to commit, embrace, and pursue your Empty Nest life. Depending on your age and when your last child leaves, you will have, on average, ten to fifteen years as an empty nester before you enter the next phase of life, retirement. And as luck would have it, retirement is just an extension of your Empty Nest Opportunities in that it will be a similar transition, providing you with even more free time. Time itself isn't the Empty Nest Advantage; it's what you do with it.

In the next chapter, we will explore time and discover the specific opportunities you can pursue to live up to the promise of fulfillment, excitement, and fun. Are you excited? Do you feel it? This is only the beginning.

Let's create your blueprint.

CHAPTER 12 KEY POINTS

- After years of prioritizing parenting over all else, your Empty Nest Opportunities are all about you.

- You are a fantastic person with unique qualities and characteristics, compliments, and an endless list of things to be grateful for.

- You have decided to commit, embrace, and pursue your best Empty Nest life.

- Your Empty Nest Advantage is time. And you are dedicated to making the most of it.

> "The greatest adventure is to explore who you are."

CHAPTER THIRTEEN

Create Your Blueprint

Part 1

IF OUR BIGGEST Empty Nest Opportunity is time, then let's take time itself and build our Empty Nest Blueprint. Leveraging information from the research and data I have collected, I have found seven major categories of opportunities that single empty nesters can experience as they transition into a "you-focused" phase of life.

The Opportunity Categories

The Empty Nest Opportunity

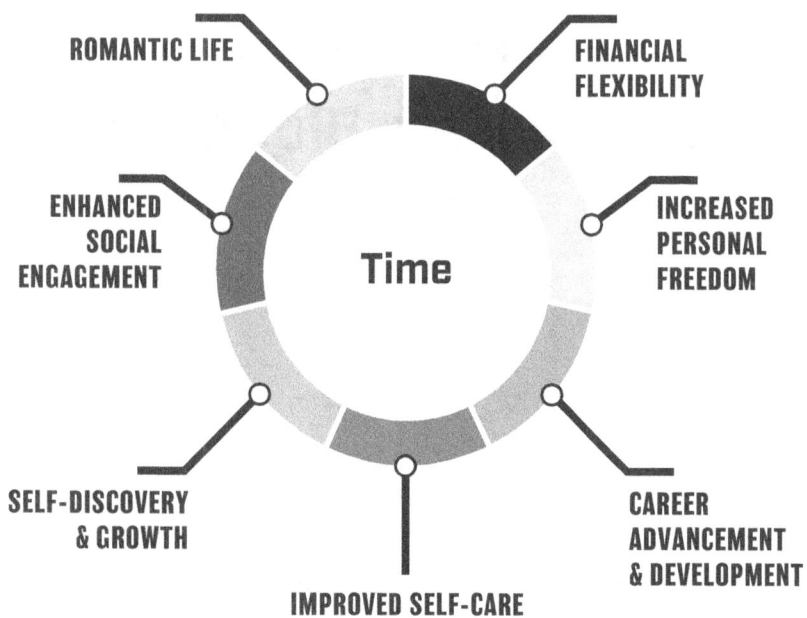

1. Increased Personal Freedom

As single parents regain significant amounts of time previously devoted to parenting responsibilities, they can focus on themselves, pursue personal interests, and engage in activities they may have put on hold while raising their children. The daily decision-making process becomes a personal preference versus having to weigh the consideration of another. Independence is abundant without the prior level of parental responsibility.

Single parents may also have more freedom and flexibility because they can be more spontaneous with routines, make plans, and re-engage with personal interests and hobbies.

2. Self-Discovery and Growth

With the children out of the house, single parents have the opportunity for personal growth, self-discovery, and new challenges outside their parent role. They can reconnect with aspects of themselves that the demands of parenting may have overshadowed. This transition frees up mental and emotional energy, which can lead to a deeper understanding of their values, interests, and aspirations beyond being parents.

3. Enhanced Social Engagement

With more time and energy, single parents can invest in socializing and connecting with friends, family, and the community. In multiple survey answers, reconnecting with friends is the highest priority in this category. Reconnecting or connecting with others has the added benefit of providing a more robust support system, fostering a sense of belonging and connection.

4. Career Advancement and Development

I hate to say, "You get to work more." However, with fewer parental responsibilities at home, single parents may be able to focus more on career goals and pursue opportunities for advancement or professional development. They can devote extra time and energy to their work, potentially leading to increased job satisfaction and earning potential. Conversely, this time could also be used to explore other career opportunities, take on an entrepreneurial endeavor, or explore professional development that may not have been possible before.

5. Improved Self-Care

With more free time and fewer daily demands, self-care often improves. Single parents can prioritize their health and well-being, both physically and mentally. Engaging in regular exercise, practicing self-care routines, and seeking support for their emotional needs leads to greater overall happiness and fulfillment. This is an opportunity to let go of daily child-rearing stress, problem-solving, and worries. Doing this can free a single parent to focus on relaxation, nutrition, and rest, combating burnout and fatigue.

6. Romantic Life

Fifty percent of the single parents I surveyed mentioned dating again or pursuing a romantic relationship as a planned activity once their child leaves the house. The same percentage was true for parents whose child had already left the home. More free time, more private time, and the absence of having to introduce someone else (a child) into a dating relationship were some of the stated factors in single parents finding themselves more open to exploring romantic relationships or rekindling connections with past partners. This is an opportunity to build new romantic relationships or nurture existing ones, bringing joy, companionship, and emotional support during this stage of life.

7. Financial Flexibility

Although the data is mixed, some single parents experience fewer financial obligations once their children leave the nest. From no longer paying child support, children living financially independently, or potentially college costs being covered by other means, single parents may experience greater financial freedom and stability. From a budgeting perspective, single parents may find themselves in a position where they can now allocate resources toward their needs and desires. This may include saving more for retirement, spending money on pursuing new experiences, or investing in personal growth.

Now that we know what the Empty Nest Opportunities are due to your free time, let's take a moment to ground ourselves by looking back at the past and the present to better understand the opportunities we have prioritized or haven't.

Exercise 1–Your Priorities

Directions: In the following table, think about each Empty Nest Opportunity and fill out the corresponding box to the degree to which this opportunity has been a priority or focus area during the first two phases of your life. Again, you are rating "to the degree'" in which you focused on this both as an adult before you became a parent and separately while you have been actively parenting (now or up to becoming an empty nester). To capture the nuance of the questions, we will use a degree scale of:

Rarely: You did this very little or not at all.

Occasionally: You did this sometimes but not frequently.

Frequently: You did this often or a lot.

Start: Take a quick moment to reflect on each opportunity and rate how much you focused on this during each phase.

OPPORTUNITY	PRE-PARENTING FOCUS	PARENTING FOCUS
Exercised Personal Freedom		
Investing in Self-Discovery and Growth		
Practiced Enhanced Social Engagement		
Focused on Career Advancement and Development		
Prioritized Self-Care		
Focused on Your Romantic Life		
Focused on Financial Flexibility/Stability		

How did you do? Are there any surprises? Do you see any patterns? In the spirit of openness, here is my assessment.

OPPORTUNITY	PRE-PARENTING FOCUS	PARENTING FOCUS
Exercised Personal Freedom	*Frequently*	*Occasionally*
Investing in Self-Discovery and Growth	*Occasionally*	*Frequently*
Practiced Enhanced Social Engagement	*Frequently*	*Occasionally*
Focused on Career Advancement and Development	*Occasionally*	*Frequently*
Prioritized Self-Care	*Occasionally*	*Rarely*
Focused on Your Romantic Life	*Frequently*	*Occasionally*
Focused on Financial Flexibility/Stability	*Occasionally*	*Frequently*

Reviewing my scoring, I realized that three things dropped from frequently to occasionally. My freedom, social engagement, and romantic life decreased when I became a parent. Self-care dropped from occasionally to rarely. The things that went up for me were self-discovery, career and professional development, and financial flexibility. Each of our grids will be unique, but it's pretty clear I focused on work and things that could help me develop in my career. It's also apparent I deprioritized some relationships and personal health and had less individual freedom.

Completing this exercise and summarizing my results helped me understand my changes and choices. If you look back at your grid and summarize it, what story does it tell? Remember, the point of this exercise isn't self-criticism but instead gaining an understanding of the past.

Now that we have a clear picture of where we have been and where we are today, let's turn the tide and focus on what we want moving forward. As an empty nester, you will be given the gift of time. What do you want to do with that time?

Exercise 2 – Your Empty Nest Focus

Directions: The following table is the same as in the last exercise. First, we are going to note what our current state is. You can copy your "parenting focus" column from the prior exercise. If you feel your priorities have changed since actively parenting, for example, if your child has already left the nest, or you have recently undergone a life change, feel free to reassess your current state. Once you complete your current column, complete your Empty Nest column. This is what you want to focus on in the future and to what degree you want to focus on it. Essentially, this column will be your response to the Empty Nest Opportunities you have reviewed. The scale will stay the same with a subtle "future action" focus. This is the revised scale.

Rarely: You don't wish to focus on this in your Empty Nest future.

Occasionally: You want to do this sometimes but not frequently in your Empty Nest future.

Frequently: You want to focus on this often during your Empty Nest future.

Start: Take a quick moment to reflect on each opportunity and rate how much you focus on this now and want to in the future. Start ranking.

OPPORTUNITY	CURRENT	EMPTY NEST
Exercising Personal Freedom		
Investing in Self-Discovery and Growth		
Practicing Enhanced Social Engagement		
Focusing on Career Advancement and Development		
Prioritizing Self-Care		
Focusing on Your Romantic Life		
Focusing on Financial Flexibility/Stability		

Was it hard to choose what opportunities you wanted to explore in your Empty Nest future? Again, I'll share and summarize my choices.

OPPORTUNITY	CURRENT	EMPTY NEST
Exercising Personal Freedom	*Occasionally*	*Frequently*
Investing in Self-Discovery and Growth	*Frequently*	*Frequently*
Practicing Enhanced Social Engagement	*Occasionally*	*Frequently*
Focusing on Career Advancement and Development	*Frequently*	*Rarely*
Prioritizing Self-Care	*Rarely*	*Frequently*
Focusing on Your Romantic Life	*Occasionally*	*Frequently*
Focusing on Financial Flexibility/Stability	*Frequently*	*Frequently*

It may or may not come as a surprise, but I want it all. Correction: My work advancement and "professional career" are not high priorities. However, my self-discovery and writing growth are highly important to me. Five of my opportunities changed from the current state to the future. Based on the data I have gathered from single empty nesters, some of the opportunities won't interest everyone. For example, many single empty nesters are pretty content with their romantic lives, are comfortable with their social engagements, or may deprioritize career advancement at this stage. As with all these exercises, there is no right or wrong or personal judgment. I hope you have at least four or five opportunities you "frequently" wish to focus on moving forward.

The point of this exercise is for you to realize the opportunities that lie before you as a single empty nester. In the last chapter, you also decided to commit, embrace, and pursue your best Empty Nest life. This is your future. Remember the great person we complimented three times in the last chapter? That person was you, and you deserve every opportunity you want. These opportunities are the exact things that will make your best Empty Nest future come true.

Going Deeper

Although I like the seven opportunity categories we have reviewed, and each contains specific examples of actions, we need more specificity as to what exactly we will do while pursuing each opportunity. It's one thing to tell yourself, "I want to do more self-care," but it's much better to "Start practicing yoga." To that end, we need to get into more detail before we complete our blueprint and create our plans. Let's dive one level down and borrow the grid we used in chapter 11 when discussing depriotization. This time, the grid doesn't represent what we have deprioritized but rather twenty-eight items we may want to pursue. This exercise will be quick and easy.

Exercise 3–Potential Activities

Directions: On the following grid circle, highlight, or note any of the twenty-eight activities that you would like to do more of during your Empty Nest future. If the words in a box resonate, interest you, or seem needed or necessary (like health), check that box. Equally as important, if any words give you a sense of happiness, excitement, and fun, check those too.

Physical health	Time with friends	Romantic relationships / dating	Fitness / exercise
Time with extended family	Pursuing hobbies and interests	Mental health	Sleep
Career Advancement	Travel and vacations	Eating healthy	Social activities and outings
Self-care routines and pampering	Professional development	Household chores/ organization	Financial investment/retirement
Educational pursuits / academic goals	Personal time for relaxation	Non-child based - volunteer work	Personal purchases or luxuries
Personal goals/aspirations	Non-child based community involvement	Home improvement/projects or renovation	Reading / arts and crafts
Attending social events	Annual checkups (dentist, doctor, etc.)	Paying off debt/ emergency fund	Personal appearance (haircuts, clothes, style)

How many activities do you have in total? Are you starting to envision what you can do in your future? Are you beginning to see how you can spend your Empty Nest days ahead? I won't share my grid, but nineteen of the twenty-eight activities resonated with me.

If we took the time to dive into each box and detail all the actions we could take within each statement, we would have pages and pages of ideas. This isn't something we can do in this book, but it is something you can do on your own. And like any long-term planning exercise, it would be worth your time. Even though this section is titled "Going Deeper," I think it would be an injustice not to blow out one specific activity category/box. Together, we will take on one activity that should be a cornerstone of your Empty Nest future: social activities and outings. This exercise requires a paper pad, pen, or computer. This one will get big, unlike all the other exercises thus far, where you could write in the book or mentally note your thoughts. Get ready to get excited about the endless possibilities of fun you have available to you in your Empty Nest future. Are you prepared to write on something? Here we go!

Exercise 4—Future Activities

We will break this brainstorming exercise into four parts to create the most extensive future opportunity list for your social activities and outings. Although it sounds like more work, we can make a more comprehensive list of ideas and possibilities by doing four separate brainstorming prompts.

Directions: Do nothing more than write a header titled "Future Activities." I've included three brainstorming prompts. Write as much as you can after reading each prompt. Only move on to the next prompt when you fully exhaust that answer.

Start: Go!

List your current interests and what you like to do. Everything you can think of.

List things you are good at and enjoy but don't do. For example, you are good at crafts, woodworking, horseshoes, and singing, but you have no outlet for them today.

List things you like, are good at, and have enjoyed in the past but don't do today. For example, I like cycling, painting, and playing poker, but I haven't done that much.

How'd it go? I hope you have generated a list of activities wholly focused on you. The list you just created will be the foundation for future activities you can pursue. Are you excited? Be proud of what you have thus far. However, there is no need to worry if the list isn't that big. This fourth and final brainstorming exercise is where your list becomes amazing.

A Quick Public Service Announcement

Before the final exercise, I wanted to share a public service announcement with you. You likely have an additional list we won't create during this exercise. This is a list of activities you have avoided and are not interested in. This is completely okay. For example, if you don't want to do pottery, learn bridge, or sing karaoke, you could not care less about professional tennis. We all have our activity preferences, and you shouldn't do anything you dislike. However, in chapter 12, you committed to change in your Empty Nest future. There was a time in my life, or perhaps many times in my past, where I defaulted to no when presented with an opportunity to have fun, connect, or experience something. I wouldn't accept an offer if I weren't initially interested. This is a horrible default. I have realized over time after being confronted with this "default to no" trait that it only isolated me from potential fun. Further, what I discovered once I started defaulting to yes is that, much more often than not, I ended up enjoying the monster truck rally, the band I never heard of, learning how to play Gloomhaven, and even going to watch professional tennis. So here is another promise I'd like you to make. If you have an opportunity to do something you might naturally say no to or not prefer, I ask that you make an exception if your child, a romantic partner or date, or a friend likes to do it. In these instances, we will embrace our power to change and at least try pottery, watch tennis with a friend, or poorly sing a Miley Cyrus song on a karaoke date. Again, your Empty Nest phase is about you, but to grow, connect, and expand our social activities and outings, don't just default to no like I used to. Look at every activity, invite, or social interaction as an opportunity to have fun.

Now you will see how the small list of things turns into hundreds or—I kid you not—thousands of activities we can do in our lifetime. Ready? Let's discover the unknown.

Exercise 4.1 – Your Endless Future Activities

Create a list of things you haven't done or thought of doing. I know what you are saying now: "How do I list things I don't know?" Although this seems difficult, if not impossible, it's the easiest brainstorming session yet. You can steal from me for this brainstorm and use whatever references you have. Trust me, the five-minute investment in time will set you up for years to come. You may also find you can spend hours on this exercise, adding more and more to your list as time passes.

This is how I quickly came up with over a hundred ideas of things I could do in the future as an empty nester, which then turned into over a thousand.

Directions: Do the following five things right now:

Google "top fifty things to do in your city/state/county." Add words like "free" or "low cost" to refine the list.

Go to TripAdvisor and check out the "top things to see" in your city or nearby cities. Essentially, act like a tourist looking up your town for a vacation.

Go to Groupon. It is not necessary to purchase a bunch of Groupons, but what you will find on Groupon is an endless list of potential local things you can do that you would never in a million years think of doing. For example, glass blowing, horse riding, painting, kayaking, dancing, arcades, brewery tours, wine tasting, art classes, ax throwing, Segway tours, etc.. There are more ideas on this platform than you could ever imagine.

Look into local, state, and national parks near you (or farther away)—there are many things to explore (on foot, by bike, or by car).

Look up local venues (local theaters, concert venues, and clubs) and subscribe to their email lists. Additionally, subscribe to a few "weekly things to do/what is happening in my area" email lists. If you search those two prompts, you will likely find several newsletters for your area. Subscribe and unsubscribe over time to find suitable target activities for you.

Did you do it? At the very least, even if your wi-fi went down, you have the twelve ideas I used as an example in number three. I hope you are now sitting on a list of more activities you can do. Some activities are expensive, such as concerts, plays, travel, and attending sports; however, several expensive activities have cheaper options (last-minute/discount tickets). You may not be in the front row, but you can still have a fun and quality overall experience alone or with someone else. And, of course, many of my favorite activities are very cheap or free (hiking, playing games, state parks, visiting a bookstore). My point is that there is much to do on anyone's budget.

But wait, you're not done. If you followed the five prompts, you should easily have over a hundred ideas. That's nothing! In the next section, your list will expand into the thousands.

Activity Bonanza

You have done it. You have an extensive list of activities you can do. Congratulations! These activities are how you will embrace your best Empty Nest life. This is one way you can find happiness, fun, and excitement in your life. You will quickly see that excitement comes back into your life when you have new things to do and fun things to look forward to. Your Friday nights, Saturdays, or Sunday afternoons can be sprinkled with new experiences.

After completing Exercise 4.1, I folded in my list from Exercise 3. My combined list had over two hundred activities I could do, and I could easily introduce them into my newfound free time and weekends. It included all four brainstorming exercises.

Here is where things get a little crazy. Many of the activities on my list weren't one-time things but topics such as sports, plays, concerts, parks, and hikes. Stepping back, each of these activities is a never-ending or rolling list. For example, California has 280 state parks, and any Major League Baseball team near you plays eighty-one home games a year. Those two ideas alone provide 361 places or events you could visit and attend. If you were to add your local parks and national parks, your numbers would grow. Then add a neighboring minor league baseball team's home schedule (75 home games), and 361 places quickly become 500 outings.

Similarly, there are countless concerts and live music events within reach of almost every city in the United States. Music alone is one activity with more live events than you could ever attend. Side note: many are free. Looking at only museums, landmarks, and outdoor trails, I found hundreds of places I could visit that were close to home. Everything from nature to tourist destinations and "must-see" places were present in my surrounding community.

The outcome of Exercise 4.4 became an endless list of brainstorming activities and places I could explore for years to come. Even more compelling, some of the activities on the list have become recurring highlights or traditions that I enjoy on a regular or semi-regular basis.

I am not saying a list of activities will guarantee an Empty Nest life of fun, excitement, and joy. But you are building your blueprint to live your best Empty Nest life. And we are combating the deprioritization of connection, fun, and excitement you may have neglected while raising a child. We took just one box out of twenty-eight, social activities and outings, and created an endless list of things for you to do and see in the future. There are twenty-seven other boxes on the grid, and quite frankly, numerous other boxes that may pertain to you that I didn't create. Your blueprint is composed of the list you just built and the lists of the other activities we outlined that you can build upon. If you do the same thing we did for the physical health box, you will have an endless list of things you could do to improve that aspect of your future. Again, your Empty Nest opportunities are endless. Thank you for deeply diving with me and exploring your fun-filled future. In the next chapter, we will discuss what you can harness to ensure individual success and then move into creating your plans. Congratulations on doing the work. Feel confident and excited that you are well on your way to setting yourself up for Empty Nest success.

In the next chapter, we will discuss what you can harness to ensure individual success and then move on to creating your blueprint plans. Congratulations on your work.

CHAPTER 13 KEY POINTS

- The most significant Empty Nest Opportunity you have is time.

- Time allows you to make future life choices and explore the seven categories of opportunity

- Your Empty Nest Blueprint brings excitement, joy, and fun back into your life.

- Your Empty Nest Blueprint draws from activities you explore to realize your best Empty Nest future.

"Your child's life will be filled with fresh experiences. It's good if yours is as well."

—DR. MARGARET RUTHERFORD

CHAPTER FOURTEEN

It's Achievable

BY COMPLETING THE exercises and building your blueprint so far, you have discovered opportunities to prioritize yourself in the future. Your inventory of activities combined with exploration of each topic area on your grid builds upon things you can start doing now. This is your blueprint for Empty Nest success. I realize incorporating new activities, reflecting on all actions you can take, and deciding to change aspects of yourself can seem overwhelming. Frankly, it is overwhelming. But what you have done thus far is very significant. The work you have put in over the last two chapters has provided you with a blueprint of possibilities

for the second half of your life. Remember, this is a long-term implementation, so you can relax knowing you have time to implement everything you have discovered. I also want to set expectations that your discoveries and actions are not "light-switch" actions. This means you can't be expected to do everything right, practice yoga daily, take up new hobbies, learn the guitar, or change everything all at once. The only change you need to make immediately is the decision to want to change and embrace the best Empty Nest life! The effort and outcomes will happen as long as you keep your realization of embracing your Empty Nest Opportunities at the forefront. Each action you take for yourself will compound and break the routine of not prioritizing yourself. Combining all the mini moments of self-love, exploration, and fun will add to a fulfilling future.

Anticipation

Let's quickly summarize your Empty Nest Opportunity blueprint thus far. You have adopted a "you-first" mindset by committing to reprioritize yourself; become empowered to change the routine you may have fallen into while raising children; and started to chart a fun and active future for yourself through endless activities.

Your Empty Nest Blueprint has taken shape, and you have done much to be proud of. All the work you completed in the last few chapters involves things you can do to strengthen yourself and proactively transition into an Empty Nest life. The final piece of making the most of your Empty Nest Opportunities is to take some time to focus on your child and yourself.

One unique fact about your Empty Nest experience is that you can anticipate and prepare for the transition. Moreover, by channeling your resilience and focusing on the positives that lie ahead, you can dictate the experience you want and create the Empty Nest Opportunities you desire. This chapter will outline how you can control your Empty Nest experience by leveraging anticipation, preparation, and resilience.

Childbirth and becoming a parent is challenging. Graduating can be anxiety-ridden. The best-planned vacation can include stressful moments. Conversely, each of those events can also be some of the most incredible experiences and memories you have in your lifetime. One of the advantages of any upcoming or planned event is you can look forward to that experience. In the prior examples—your child's birth, your graduation, or your latest vacation—you likely anticipated the event as being filled with excitement and positivity. In fact, not only was the event a positive experience but the journey and planning that led up to each experience were also positive. The same can be true for your Empty Nest experience. As you plan to become an empty nester, the events, actions, and positive outlook you create can make the journey amazing.

As you plan to become an empty nester, the events, actions, and positive outlook you create can make the journey amazing.

Creating your Empty Nest Blueprint is about embracing all the positive outcomes that will happen as you journey into an Empty Nest lifestyle. Anticipation is about looking forward to something, and it's almost always positive. Let's set you up for the best Empty Nest outcome by anticipating all the positives that lie ahead for you and your child.

Your Child

I'm reasonably sure most parents don't sit down the day their children are born and write out a list of goals they have as parents. I can further assume most parents don't write down what kind of life they want for their children. Raising a child from infant to young adult is more experiential than a to-do list of stated goals. But if we truly think about it, there are a lot of unstated goals most parents have. The American Psychological Association states, "Parenting practices worldwide share three major goals: ensuring children's health and safety, preparing children for life as productive adults, and transmitting cultural values."

Good news! If you reach the point where your child is off to college, entering the workforce, or striking out on their own, it is safe to say you have achieved those goals from the APA. This next stage in your child's life is one where they will leverage the hard work and guidance and the struggles and successes you have fostered and experienced with them. Your dedication and support have paid off as your child moves toward their next stage of growth and development.

Take a moment to think about your growth and experience when you ventured out of your parents' home. Was it not an adventure of excitement and opportunity as you flexed your independence? Were you excited about your freedom? Were you excited about the ability to make your daily choices and live independently? There is jubilation in personal growth. Now your child gets to live this experience for themselves. They will learn to manage their newfound freedom and experience their life choices through trial and error. They decide when and what to eat, when to sleep and get up, what activities they choose to explore, and with whom they want to spend time. Just as you did, your child will grow by charting their day, developing their experiences, and accomplishing goals. They will embrace their privacy, develop a greater sense of freedom, and subconsciously put all the lessons and values you instilled in them to the test. I wouldn't necessarily expect a thank-you note, but your child will leverage everything you gave them as a parent.

This is a fantastic time for your child. It is also a testament to your parenting and hard work. It is a time when you can experience the joy and excitement of life through them while being proud of your accomplishment in preparing them for this next phase in their life. You have done an incredible job. It wasn't easy. Have gratitude for the journey you have been on with them. Have excitement about both their own and your future with them. Use both of these things—gratitude and excitement—to chart your next phase in life.

Pulling In Others

Regardless of how close you are to another person, you cannot know all the feelings and emotions they will experience during their Empty Nest journey. That being said, when exposed to someone taking this journey, you can dedicate yourself to helping them through it and work toward making their transition as positive as possible. It is likely that, by reading this book, you have given more thought to becoming an empty nester than your family, neighbor, or friend has unless they also read this book. You understand the US averages, the syndrome, and the four Ds. You are aware of the downsides of this phase, and you have created a positive future for yourself. One of the best things you can do for your Empty Nest transition is to help others focus on the positives of their past, present, and future journey.

The positives for any empty nester are endless. You have done the work in chapter 13 to create your blueprint. You can use the knowledge you have gained and what you have planned to help others prepare for themselves or join you in your fun-filled future. And you can start right now. You don't have to wait for your child to graduate from high school and leave to implement activities with others. Use your brainstorming skills to set some goals in the near and long term, including those of family and friends. Ideally, the sooner you start anticipating and implementing your Empty Nest strategy, the sooner you will enjoy newfound possibilities.

Remember the example of childbirth, graduation, and vacation? The anticipation of the event can be equal to the joy derived from experiencing the event. Even if you are in a situation where your children are several years away from leaving or, on the other side of the spectrum, if they have already left your house, you have an opportunity right now to reset and focus on the anticipation and excitement of sharing your Empty Nest future with others.

You

All the experiential examples we have covered in this book aren't tied to a specific day but a journey. With each activity you have identified, you have created the opportunity to do three things: relish the anticipation, embrace the experience as you have it, and reflect on it later as a positive life memory. Whether it's as simple as planning to see a movie this weekend or becoming an empty nester, the three stages of the opportunity apply.

This book outlines some of the negative aspects of becoming an empty nester. I hope that you can successfully arm yourself with a strategy to avoid a negative outcome by understanding the pitfalls and roadblocks ahead.

Your Empty Nest Opportunities are about understanding the situation and leveraging the opportunity you have in front of you. With this understanding, you can apply what you know and plan to benefit your child, family, friends, and most importantly yourself. At this point, you should feel excited for your child. It's not the only feeling you are experiencing, but you are aware of the gamut of emotions and can master them. You should be excited for your friends. You can enlist them to get excited about participating in your future of fun. It would be best if you now got excited about your future as an empty nester. As we have learned, it's entirely up to you. Let's review why you should feel this way:

- You are knowledgeable, prepared, and get what becoming an empty nester is all about. You are in an envious position!
- You have successfully raised your child to the point where they are ready to move out independently. Congratulations!
- You have reviewed your priorities and are prepared to embrace a "you-focused" future. Fantastic!
- You have worked on a blueprint to create the future you want. Amazing!

- You are aware of and can leverage all the benefits of becoming an empty nester: more free time, interests, reconnection, fun experiences, planned excitement, less stress, less work, gratitude, and the opportunity to plan and implement your desired future.

All the positives of your Empty Nest journey stack on top of each other, creating endless possibilities. These positives pave the way for your success and happiness. Since you are at the center of your own Empty Nest journey, it is in your power to create your best future. I am excited to tell you that you are already well on your way!

Resilience

You have set a tone for your Empty Nest Opportunities by working toward a positive future. You understand what the journey can be like and what you want yours to be. You are anticipating positive outcomes for all involved. If anticipation sets the tone for your Empty Nest Opportunities, then resilience is the instrument you play. We know that there is no magic pill one can take to make the negative feelings go away. Even the most positive people who embrace all the good of their Empty Nest journey will experience some negative emotions. A key opportunity to ensure a more positive outcome is to leverage your resilience. Resilience is one of the most powerful personal tools at your disposal, and it will allow you to manage, limit, and counter any lingering negative emotions.

> **If anticipation sets the tone for your
> Empty Nest Opportunities, then
> resilience is the instrument you play.**

Each of us lives in a world filled with multiple challenges. Most challenges and jobs are more demanding when only one person does it. Being a single parent is the quintessential example of this. You have faced adversity, setbacks, and challenges while raising your child, yet you have had to channel your resiliency. The definition of resilience fits perfectly into your Empty Nest Opportunities. Resilience is "the ability of a person to adjust to or recover readily from illness, adversity, or major life changes." Your resilience harnesses your inner strength to rebound from a setback or challenge. Each of our life stories contains examples of challenges and resiliency. These are the times when we have worked to overcome issues at work, in relationships, in our environment, or within ourselves. Resilience is not a cure-all for life's problems. However, channeling your resilience can allow you to see past a problem, learn from overcoming a challenge, and enjoy life more with less stress.

As a future empty nester, you channel your resilience by creating realistic plans and goals, carrying out your plans, and being able to identify and healthily manage your feelings and impulses. You can see the major life change ahead, and you are working toward the best outcome. Does this sound relatable to your Empty Nest Opportunities?

If you are concerned that becoming an empty nester will take an emotional toll on you, you can become more resilient. One way to do this is to anticipate your emotions and work toward building up your resilience. This is the best way to stave off depression, sadness, loss, or loneliness. Resilience will not stop the negative feelings from happening, but it will help you "adjust to" or "recover readily." If the thought of your child leaving the home has you worried, fearful, or dreading the day, here is an example of how to apply your resiliency.

- **Know what is going to happen.** Your child is leaving the home.
- **Know what it will entail.** There will be a process of planning, getting ready, and then implementing that plan.
- **Know who you can leverage to support you through this situation.** Get help from your family, friends, or another support group who have experienced the same thing.
- **Be confident you have a plan.** You have thought through the short-term situations and have planned a long-term, fun-filled Empty Nest future.
- **Know that you will get through it.** You have prepared yourself with knowledge of an Empty Nest

transition. You know what you may experience, and you are ready for it.

These points will not only help build up your resilience to your child leaving but to any situation where you may have dread, anxiety, or fear. Experiencing emotions such as sadness, loss, or loneliness is perfectly normal and healthy. Your Empty Nest transition will involve letting go, and sometimes that comes with anxiety and sadness. It's okay to cry, be sad, and experience many emotions during this or any other life event. The purpose of this section is not to stop any negative feelings from happening but rather to see the benefits as well as to use your coping mechanisms to ensure a positive overall experience versus experiencing a debilitating trigger toward situational depression. Resilience will help you adjust and recover quickly. Anticipation will help you focus on your positive future.

Single-Parent Empty Nest Advice

The last question I asked in the survey I conducted was: "What advice would you give to another single empty nester?" Here are ten responses I received that represent the major themes from all of the responses: What advice would you give to another single empty nester?

- Give them space to grow. By doing so, your relationship with them will strengthen and grow.

- Enjoy yourself. If there is ever a time to do so, this is that time.
- Feel your feelings. It's okay to grieve, be sad, or even feel a little lost.
- Start planning for your empty nest journey. Find interests and hobbies that will replace daily contact with your children.
- Try to remember that, when the plane loses pressure, you should put your oxygen mask on first.
- Don't let your social life become an empty nest, too.
- If you are not healthy and caring for yourself first, you cannot adequately help others, including your child(ren).
- Be supportive to your children. Let them know you're proud of them and always there for them.
- Keep your faith. Let it support and guide you.
- Don't be afraid to date again. If you're open to it, put yourself out there!

What I love about these responses isn't the originality of one but the beauty of the whole. Have you ever been in a group where everyone talks about their favorite things, such as a movie or ice cream, and as each person answers, you say to yourself, "Oh yeah, I forgot about that movie. I loved *The Iron Giant*." or "Damn, I love butter brickle ice cream too." For a single empty nester, each response and piece of advice is like a stepping stone, and when all the stones are put together, we have a path to follow. These themes aren't new, but they do, in totality, capture the shared experience of a single empty nester.

The Empty Nest Opportunities Are Achievable

My Empty Nest Opportunities started when I decided to take an introspective look at my future after my first child left. I decided to reflect, focus, and find a way to take action to avoid the many pitfalls others have fallen into—specifically, the Empty Nest Threats. My goal was to pivot to a new trajectory, a future where fun, excitement, and joy became more of a constant state. I read and researched everything I could find, which led me to discover that becoming an empty nester is a worthy and underrated topic for both single and married empty nesters.

The last three chapters, starting with the Empty Nest Opportunities, summarize the themes discovered and the work needed for a parent to create their best Empty Nest future. I shifted my mindset to a "fun-filled" future focus. I changed my perspective and found ways to counter the routines I was stuck in. I anticipated my Empty Nest transition's emotional and physical impact and knew I would be more resilient with a plan. Everything I have shared helped me or has helped single parents combat the Empty Nest Threats. I believe the exercises, self-exploration, and blueprint can also help you.

Today, I am living the Empty Nest dream. I wake up every day choosing to focus on my future and the things I can get excited about. These are fun, exciting, relaxing, learning, enjoyable, and self-caring activities and actions I have planned for myself. Every day, I work to improve in the areas where I have deprioritized myself. All of this does not mean my life is perfect. It is not. There are interpersonal struggles, financial surprises, moments of exhaustion, and times when I don't feel aligned. My goal has never been to have a perfect life. In my view, a perfect life is unachievable. Creating an Empty Nest Blueprint, however, is within our reach. You can focus, plan, and make the next thirty-plus years after your children leave fantastic. You, too, can get excited about your future. You can have your best Empty Nest life.

The next chapter, titled "Your Plan for You," pulls together everything you have done so far and prepares you for your future. It's time to put the finishing touches on your blueprint. It's time to create your Empty Nest plans.

CHAPTER 14 KEY POINTS

🖊 By anticipating the roadblocks on your Empty Nest journey, you can use your resilience to overcome obstacles.

🖊 Take the advice of your single-parent Empty Nest peers.

🖊 Your Empty Nest Opportunities are achievable. You are well on your way!

There are dreamers and there are planners; the planners make their dreams come true."

—EDWIN LOUIS COLE

CHAPTER FIFTEEN

Your Plan for You
Blueprint Part 2

YOU HAVE JOURNEYED from Empty Nest Syndrome to Empty Nest solutions. You have looked back at your past and understand where you are today. You have previewed the Empty Nest Threats and grabbed hold of the Opportunities. By now, you are aware of both the pitfalls and pain points as well as the promise and possibilities of an Empty Nest journey. Through resolve, awareness, and introspection, you have decided to make your Empty Nest journey one of fulfillment, excitement, and fun.

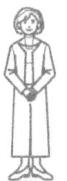

This chapter is about creating a plan for your best journey. Don't let the work associated with creating a plan cause you to pause. You are a planner, whether you believe it or not. You have planned and completed an endless list of activities, events, and actions throughout your life. Raising a child is impossible without the gift of planning, and you have leveraged that gift over and over. Now you get to put it into action for yourself.

At the end of the following two chapters, you will have at least two plans: a plan for you and a plan for your child. You may also have an "alloparent plan," which I will detail further in the pages ahead.

My wording is intentional in that each of these plans is yours, which you own and implement. Although we will explain these plans in more detail throughout, they are not a plan for your child or anyone else to execute but rather your plan for you as you interact with each audience—a subtle but important difference.

With your plans in place, you will have concrete steps, actions, and ideas to implement your Empty Nest plans. You are already on your way to creating your best Empty Nest future.

Life Planning

When you reflect on your life from a planning perspective, most planning is done in the moment. For example,

"What do you want for dinner? What are you doing Friday night? Let's take a trip to Disney World." In these examples, you desire to do something (dinner, activity, trip) and then act to achieve the goal. Most plans are decisions that take moments to achieve while other plans require more time. If we look at the example of the Africa trip, it seems like a big planning commitment. In reality, it isn't as time-consuming as you would think. Most experts recommend planning big vacations six months out and suggest you need an average of five hours' worth of planning. Although a Disney vacation is planned and is a big trip, it doesn't require nor is it considered long-term planning.

For most Americans, just a handful of activities can be classified as long-term goals or plans. Most long-term plans fall into four distinct categories:

- education
- finances
- personal development
- career planning

As luck would have it, several of these long-term categories are in the middle of one's Empty Nest journey. For example, saving money for and spending on a child's education falls within the Empty Nest timeline. Planning and saving for retirement also falls within the Empty Nest timeline. Entering one's peak earning years in one's career also falls within the Empty Nest timeline. Each of these long-term planning activities happens most intensely between the ages of forty-five and sixty.

So where does Empty Nest planning sit on a planning timeline? Ideally, one would be thinking about a plan concerning their Empty Nest status throughout their forties. But, practically speaking, most people have other things on their minds when their children are young. The next best time to develop an Empty Nest plan would be when your child's departure is within your line of sight. Parents with a departing child in high school seems to be the sweet spot. That gives you one to four years to focus on the upcoming life change. Even a one-year timeline may seem over-optimistic for some of us to start thinking about our Empty Nest journey. Whatever the ideal timeline, take solace that being prepared to become an empty nester is akin to saving for retirement; it's never too early and never too late to start. The key isn't when but rather to become aware you need a plan and start planning.

My Planning Story

I realized that I was a planner at an early age. This realization didn't happen because of some gene in my DNA, but rather, it stemmed from the things I wanted in my childhood. My parents did an admirable job raising four children and accomplishing this feat on a schoolteacher's salary. However, the income level of our household dictated that, if the four of us children wanted things such as clothing, a car, or a college degree, we would have to pay for it on our own. The only solution to achieving these goals was to work, save, and plan. Knowing this, my siblings and I planned and saved for the clothes we wanted, our first cars, and college.

Beyond saving, I have always had an aptitude for planning. I enjoyed planning activities, parties, travel, and events. My internal reasoning seemed to default to "How else will I ever achieve my bucket list of dreams if I don't plan for them?" A great example is naming my son Everest. There is a longer story here, but when Everest was born, I knew I would have to take him to see his namesake someday. This idea/plan started when he was born. Fifteen years later, I booked a trekking trip to the Mt. Everest base camp for the two of us, and then I trained for about a year to be physically where I wanted to be for the trek. A nineteen-day Himalayan hiking trip requires a lot of planning, the right gear and clothing, physical preparation, and logistics. The trip was amazing, and part of the reason it went so well was due to all of the preplanning. As a parent, I have always been drawn toward short- and long-term plans while my wife would take care of the day-to-day plans. Although this was never formally agreed to, it seemed to work for us. When I hear stories from a single parent about the time and effort it takes to do the day-to-day planning, raise children, and maintain short- and long-term plans, I am humbled. For the record, I realize that some of my inclinations for planning throughout my life were about control of money while other drivers were about the love of a good plan. I liked anticipating what would happen in unknown situations, so I knew what to expect. In cases where there wasn't a plan,

I often found myself uncomfortable. It took some maturity and self-discovery to learn later in life about the magic of accepting an unplanned moment and embracing spontaneity. I have realized that some of life's best moments happen when you wander and stumble upon the unexpected.

In hindsight, planning has served me well. Not having a retirement plan, understanding your situation, or saving for something important would be foolhardy. Perhaps this better explains not only my Empty Nest realization but also why this book was written. The absence of a plan potentially lets in the negative, while having a plan builds the foundation for what you want to achieve. If you want to ensure that your Empty Nest stage in life becomes all it can be with the best possible outcome, you need a plan. Whether you are a planner like me or love "going with the flow," you need a plan for your Empty Nest Opportunities to come true.

> **If you want to ensure that your Empty Nest stage in life becomes all it can be with the best possible outcome, you need a plan.**

One Last Pitch

I hope that you don't need any convincing at this point. But just in case you are still a skeptic, I am here to tell you that you need a plan one last time. Without an Empty Nest plan, you will be at the whim of your emotions. If you believe you have complete control of the Empty Nest process and your own emotions, realize your child may be experiencing negative emotions and struggles outlined in the previous chapters. With a plan in place, you can move forward with confidence and knowledge and have more control over the Empty Nest journey as it unfolds. Your days as an empty nester aren't destined to be unknown, troublesome, and riddled with anxiety, but instead, you can prepare for a future where you and your relationships are stronger than ever.

> ### "A goal without a plan is just a wish."
> **—ANTOINE DE SAINT-EXUPÉRY**

If a goal without a plan is just a wish, then let's ensure your wishes come true by creating your plans. The great news is that, throughout this book, you have already developed your Empty Nest awareness and understanding coupled with your reflection. With these insights and some guidance, you are ready to take this next step. This section will develop your plan for yourself, your child, and your Empty Nest life. Armed with your plans, you can empathize, energize, and take action throughout your Empty Nest journey. Let's start planning for the most important person in this journey: you.

The Plan for You

The hours we spend talking to ourselves in our minds far outweigh the time we spend speaking to others. Our internal thoughts are great because they help us process our emotions, explore potential outcomes, and build awareness of our surroundings. Throughout this book, you have done each of these things. You have thought about what you have read. You have likely embraced a concept, repeated a phrase, and even dismissed a belief. This will all come together as you develop your plan for you. Your plan for you consists of three parts: awareness, anticipation, and support.

Since most learning occurs in our mind and is processed through our thoughts, our planning process starts there. You can do two things as we move forward: physically write down your plans as we go through each or mentally think through your plan as we go. Writing key points down or highlighting a sentence may work best for some; however, others prefer to think and ponder over the written word. There is no right way to move forward because our learning and planning processes are unique. Do what works for you as you develop your plans' key components. Let's go.

Part 1: Awareness

The number-one takeaway from this book, which is the backbone of each plan, is awareness. By acknowledging that being an empty nester is more than just two words assigned to you, you have already put yourself in a better position to cope with whatever comes with your change in status.

First, be aware of your emotions. How are you feeling about your journey toward becoming an empty nester? Excitement? Anxiety? Pride? Fear? Happiness? What are the emotions that you are feeling? In chapter 1, my answer was fear. I was excited and proud that my children were on a path toward independence, but at the same time, I was scared that I deprioritized essential things in my life. My concern led to the realization that, unless I changed and set a plan in place for something different, the years of a child-focused life might lead to loneliness and disconnection after my children left.

Pivoting back to you, in this part of your plan, think through your good and bad emotions. Let's complete a few quick exercises to gain more awareness.

This exercise will help you recognize your vulnerability to Empty Nest Syndrome and your emotions. Again, putting pen to paper may make this more meaningful. Let's quickly see if Empty Nest Syndrome is something you need to worry about.

Exercise 1 – Empty Nest Syndrome

Directions: Thinking back to chapter 5, do any of the Empty Nest Syndrome symptoms resonate with you? The symptoms were:

- **Loss of Identity**
- **Loss of Control**
- **Emotional Toll**
- **Relationship and Individual Stress**
- **Parenting Anxiety**

It's completely understandable if some of these topics resonate with you or if you think this could be an issue in your future.

Start: White down your symptoms.

Do you have a few? If so, take hold of their Empty Nest solution counterparts in chapter 6 and incorporate them into your plan. The solutions were:

- **Redefine Your Purpose**
- **Create Connection**
- **Seek Support**
- **Embrace Your Individual Upside**
- **Trust Your Work**

Start: If you have an identified symptom, write down how to apply the solution to your symptom.

Here is an example of one of my symptoms and what I did for this exercise:

My symptom was **Loss of Control,** and the solution was to **Create Connection.**

My application of the solution looked like this: Let go of control. Explain my expectations to my daughter. Listen to her expectations. Relinquish college grade oversight, relinquish financial control, and communicate my safety concerns and worries. Let her know I am here for her.

Do you have some symptoms identified and a solution that will help you overcome them? I sincerely hope that, if you did identify with a symptom, you have your first-draft attempt to counter it. Just like my control example, you now have a plan for that Empty Nest Syndrome symptom.

The following exercise will quickly assess your emotions during the Empty Nest stage.

Exercise 2 – Your Emotions

Directions: List each emotion (positive, negative, or somewhere in between) you believe you will feel during your Empty Nest transition. Write down everything you think/know you will feel.

Start: Create your list.

How did you do? Are you feeling good? Do you have an ample list of emotions? Let's keep going. For reference, here are four of my emotions.

I had a much longer list. For this example, I took two positive and two negative emotions on my list: sad, worried, excited, and proud. Now, go back to your list of emotions and briefly write down why you expect to or currently feel that way. Do this for each emotion.

My Example:

Sad—Because I will miss them being a big part of my daily life and routine. We have been together for eighteen years.

Worried—College is a big place, with a lot of unknowns and unknown people. I have some safety concerns about a college student's judgment, not necessarily my children but potentially others around them.

Excited—I'm excited for their new experiences, growth, and independence. This is going to be a great time in their lives.

Proud—I am proud of their hard work, success, and the person they are becoming. I am also proud of myself for helping them get to this point. Completing the this exercise will provide you with a list of emotions you can learn to embrace. Each emotion was identified by you, as was your reasoning as to why you will feel that emotion.

Your list is a valuable summary of understanding your perspective about your Empty Nest transition and the reasoning behind your thoughts. If so inclined, work toward accepting the negative feelings and then write down a counter statement of each stating the positive outcomes. For example, I countered my two negative feelings (sad and worried) by stating the positive outcomes.

Sad becomes: Focus on the positives and be happy. They are living their best life, and I now can too.

Worried becomes: They are well equipped to handle themselves. I trust them. I believe in them.

Of course, this doesn't mean I won't be sad or worried, but it does help me gain a positive perspective by seeing my feelings flipped into what I could focus on when they arise.

We just covered your emotions and feelings; now let's move on to anticipation, the new perspective of your Empty Nest life.

Part 2: Anticipation

Remember, your plan for you consists of three parts: awareness, anticipation, and support. Let's turn our focus on anticipation. In the following exercise, we will define your Empty Nest transitional life.

Exercise 3 – Your Transitional Life

Directions: Read each question and answer. Try and write at least one complete sentence for each. The more, the better.

Start:

1. How involved are you in preparing for your child's departure?
2. What are you doing with your child to prepare?
3. What are you doing for yourself to prepare?
4. What do the following days, weeks, and months look like after your child leaves?

   □ What are you doing day-to-day?
   □ What are you doing for yourself (self-care/self-love)?
   □ What is your relationship with your child like?

Did going through this help you create a mental picture of your Empty Nest life? While thinking through the questions, did you anticipate any hurdles or issues you may encounter? Additionally, did you identify exciting attributes and positive outcomes? If not, don't worry—we will do this in the next and final exercise of your plan for you.

Here is a summary of my answers in the last three exercises:

- I am involved in my child's departure (college applications, skills, financial and logistical planning).

- I realized I needed to let go of the "controlling" aspects of my active parenting. I had some natural concerns for their safety and some fear of whether they would make good decisions once away from home.
- My positive emotions were excitement for my children. At the same time, I was looking forward to anticipated calmness with less stress at home.
- I envisioned living in a child-free home, with quiet time, more personal freedom, and more one-on-one time with my spouse.
- I saw myself hiking, binge-watching shows I wanted, and doing the reading I had seemed to put off.
- I was hopeful my relationship with my child would grow as long as I focused on letting go and supporting them simultaneously.

Remember, this plan is about you. I tried my best to visualize what emotions I would experience and what my life would look like. I thought about what I would do at home, on weekends, and for myself. I also thought about what I wanted in my relationship with my children. Although I felt I had a good grasp of the practical side of my Empty Nest transition, I realized I completely forgot to build the future of my dreams. I visualized "the practical" but needed to add all "the potential" to my list.

Adding to Your List

Since starting my Empty Nest journey, I have learned a lot. Some would say enough to write a book. When I reviewed the emotions and anticipation that made up version one of my plan for myself, I realized that I had significant missing components. I ultimately left out my plan's "what could be" attributes. So much so that I had to go back to the exercise and incorporate all those items. Let me quickly explain what I mean so you don't make the same mistake I made.

This book lets you understand the different dynamics people may face when becoming an empty nester. The first part of your plan is understanding your feelings toward your Empty Nest status. You have identified your emotions and why you feel that way. You have anticipated what your Empty Nest journey will look like, both before your child leaves and after they have left. As of right now, you have a solid idea of how you believe you will feel when you become an empty nester and what your life will potentially be like. Great, let's call you "Empty Nest self-aware."

Although this is a positive step forward, my mistake initially was that my lack of imagination ultimately constrained my plan for myself. My plan should have included every positive emotion and anticipation I could think of, wanted for myself, and had the power to experience. Let's look at your plan for you with a fresh set of eyes. It should have the following things in it:

- fun
- excitement
- leisure time
- self-exploration, development, growth
- the opportunity to be healthier, happier, and closer to the ones you love
- personal fulfillment
- fulfilling relationships/connections/love

Remember, this is your plan. You own it, you define it, and you get to create it in any way you choose. Before the skeptical part of your brain starts arguing with you, realize that all the positives aren't just words or pie-in-the-sky ideas like "be happy"; they are all completely available and attainable to you. Here are some concrete examples.

You can read that book you wanted, binge-watch that show you love, reach out to friends you have lost touch with, or pursue a hobby. You can dive into nature, get into shape, and attend happy hours, concerts, or community events. You can volunteer, take classes, and rethink your career. You can anticipate an unlimited number of things you can do for yourself that you have either been neglecting, haven't had the time for, or just never thought of. You can do all of these things and more. Create your best plan for yourself. This isn't "be happy" mumbo-jumbo; it is anticipating real stuff you want to do and the action you can take. You can do it!

Exercise 3.5 – Try It Again: Your Transitional Life

Directions: Once again, you are going to read the questions you answered before and answer them. However, this time, each of your answers should incorporate at least one of the following:

- **fun**
- **excitement**
- **leisure time**
- **self-exploration, development, growth**
- **the opportunity to be healthier, happier, and closer to the ones you love**
- **personal fulfillment**
- **fulfilling relationships/connection/love**

Let's do this! Get that pen out.

Start:

1. How involved are you in preparing for your child's departure?
2. What are you doing with your child to prepare?
3. What are you doing for yourself to prepare?
4. What do the following days, weeks, and months look like after your child leaves?

    □ What are you doing day-to-day?
    □ What are you doing for yourself?

▫ What is your relationship with your child like?

How did you do? Were your answers much more positive. exciting, glorious, and fun? My second set of answers to the same questions with positive anticipation looked different. I anticipated and planned to have fun preparing for my child's departure. I was going to bond, laugh, and connect with my child. After my child left for college, I would do everything I wanted to do for myself. Everything was on the table. I was planning to incorporate all my activities into my future. I would focus on myself, my friends, my health, and my fun and support my child's independence.

The questions we looked at were the same. However, this time, we anticipated and planned for our own best plan. I hope you see the power of incorporating anticipation into your plan for you.

Part 3: Support

The final piece of your plan for you is to think through your support structure. You are not alone in your Empty Nest journey; therefore, who do you have in your corner? An easy way to get your list of names is, when faced with family drama, work issues, or difficulties in life, who are the people you confide in? Remember, in your Empty Nest life you get to choose. You know that your child will go through this transition in tandem with you, but who else do you want to join you on this journey? Even though you are the epicenter of your Empty Nest world, you can pull in countless others who have gone before you and have experienced similar concerns, anxiety, and emotions. This is an important point: just because your Empty Nest plan is all about you doesn't mean you should execute it on your own.

> **This is an important point. Just because your Empty Nest plan is about you, doesn't mean you should execute it alone.**

Think through your friends, family, and extended support group, and be open to leaning on any or all of them if you need help. Connect and share how you are doing with others to keep your mental awareness of the situation and your health at the center. Also, you may want to recruit any of them in your identified fun activities. You are the driving force behind your Empty Nest transition. You are the one who will develop the future you want. The strength of your plan and thriving through this milestone will come from you and the people you engage with. You may find the process easier and more successful if you are open to bringing others in. You don't have to do this alone.

Who I Leveraged

In support, I found that most of my Empty Nest bonding came from friends and family members who went through this before me. Being the youngest of four children, each of my siblings had already experienced their own childrens' college departures, finances, and expectations. I probed them on topics across the board, and although each parent-child situation and Empty Nest philosophy differed, I gained perspective from what they had done. I brought up the topic of departing children and marital relationships with colleagues I was close with. Again, I gained perspective by listening to their stories, rules, and struggles. I tapped into friends whose children had already left their homes before mine and asked them about being empty nesters and fostering ongoing relationships with their spouses and children.

I was amazed that whoever I asked always responded thoughtfully, engagingly, and personally to my questions. Almost everyone was willing to share their perspective. I hope you have people you can tap into and learn from, like me. My other hope is that, through this book, I have become one of the support structures you can rely on. To summarize quickly, your plan for yourself is that you are aware of your emotions and what you can become. You anticipate all of the positives that you want moving forward. You have identified the people you can draw upon if you need support. You have an excellent plan for yourself during this Empty Nest transition.

CHAPTER 15 KEY POINTS

- The first plan in your blueprint you need to create is a plan for you.

- Understanding your feelings toward becoming an empty nester, your syndrome suscep-tibility, and your anticipated outcomes lay the foundation for your plan.

- Create your plan so that it contains everything you want for yourself in your Empty Nest life.

- You are the driving force behind your Empty Nest transition, but you don't have to do it alone.

"If you fail to plan, you are planning to fail!"

—BENJAMIN FRANKLIN

CHAPTER SIXTEEN

Your Plan for Your Child

Blueprint Part 3

CONGRATULATIONS ON COMPLETING your plan for you. Feel both proud and excited that you have put yourself in a position to thrive as an empty nester. Now that your plan is set, let's create another plan to ensure you are prepared for your child's best outcome. Get excited because we will complete your plan for your child in this chapter.

338 THE EMPTY NEST BLUEPRINT FOR SINGLE PARENTS

Your Plan for Your Child

There are three parts to your plan for your child: pre-departure, communication, and your future parent-adult relationship. This plan is for you to own and execute like your own plan.

The first part of the plan centers around your child's transition out of the home. It encompasses your thoughts and expectations for your child before and after they leave the nest. This is where you articulate your expectations for your child to yourself. These expectations may focus on communication, money, grades, health, or any other responsibility you may have a continued vested interest in. This also includes some expectations and control you will forfeit once they leave.

Beyond deciding on expectations, the first part of the plan also incorporates all the pre-departure preparation you want to instill in your child: how to do laundry, cook, and pay bills online. At this point, you aren't physically doing these things with your child but rather thinking through your preparation and expectations concerning your child's departure. This is your preparation for any future actions and conversations with them. Before creating part one of your plan for your child, we need to gauge where you are in the process. As you know, we always start with our self-awareness. Briefly think about the following three topics. You can mentally think through them or write them down. In your plan for you, I asked how you felt about your Empty Nest transition. These three questions are a bit more specific:

- How do you feel toward your child? (frustration, love, tension, pride, etc.)
- How do you feel about the reality of your child leaving? (prepared, scared, excited, sad, etc.)
- How do you plan to disengage from active parenting? What specifically are you going to do or not do?

Answering these three questions will not only prepare you for their departure but also help set the stage for expectations and preparation. Let's move on.

Expectations

In chapter 9, we discussed expectations. As you may recall, my three academic expectations for my children were to show up for class, take school seriously, and graduate in four years. Remember, expectations are not rules; they are desired outcomes. And part of letting your children go is accepting that they aren't enforceable. The point of the following exercise is for you to realize your expectations and desired outcomes. Believe it or not, you likely have a lot of expectations of your child after they leave the home. You may not think you do, but this exercise may surprise you. Let's see if I'm right.

I've summarized the top ten expectations that parents have for their children once they leave the home. I have garnered these from my survey data and articles. Each of the ten issues, such as academics, can have several subtopics associated with it. For example, academics isn't just about grades. It can include courses taken, course load, study habits, and communicating with counselors and professors as subtopics. As a parent, you could have an expectation for each.

Exercise 1 – Identifying Your Expectations

Directions: Read each topic and identify if you have an expectation associated with it. If you do, write that expectation down in a single sentence. For example, for course load, "I expect Johnny to take a full course load of at least fifteen units each semester so that he graduates in four years." I also expect Johnny to "speak with a counselor or academic advisor so that he stays on track and chooses the correct required classes to graduate." These are two expectation examples under the academic topic.

Start: Ready to identify your expectations? Go.

Expectation Topics

1. Academics: grades, course load, studying, communicating with counselors and professors
2. Maturity and responsibility: managing time (balancing classes, studying, socializing, and sleep)

3. Financial responsibility: budgeting, managing a student account, part-time work
4. Healthy habits: Eating well, being active, positive self-care, and avoiding excessive distractions (partying, video games, socializing)
5. Personal safety: being aware of surroundings, looking after oneself and one's possessions, and having a plan for emergencies
6. Staying in touch: regular phone calls, texts, or video chats
7. Communicating about problems: academic struggles, roommate issues, emotional challenges
8. Building healthy relationships with roommates and classmates: dating, socialization, respect for others, and conflict resolution
9. Personal growth: exploring new interests, developing new skills, and gaining a broader worldview
10. Substance use: acceptable behavior around alcohol, drugs, and tobacco use

Upon review, I easily had ten expectations within this list. Depending on your circumstance and your child, you could easily have three or thirty. It's important to remember that these are your expectations. They are important to you for a reason. You will need to decide if each is something you want to communicate to your child or let go. The key to this exercise is that you now know explicitly what expectations you have of your child once they depart.

We'll discuss communication in the next section. But for now, let's see if we can let some of these expectations go. Letting go of an expectation doesn't mean you don't care or that your desire for an outcome will cease to exist. It also doesn't mean you won't communicate that expectation with your child. What letting go of an expectation means is that, after you have had a conversation about it and your child understands, you let go of actively trying to manage it, following up on it, or even asking your child about it. Remember, I let go of asking about grades. I let go of managing college finances (besides the money drop). I let go of my communication expectations as much as I could. There were things I didn't let go of. I didn't let go of the expectation to graduate in four years, and I continued to ask about their health. If they got sick, I would ask if they went to the medical center, and I would call and follow up until they felt better. When they came home on breaks, I would ensure they visited the eye doctor or dentist or had a checkup throughout their college years.

Exercise 1.5 – Your Expectations

Directions: Go back through your list of expectations for your child and see if you have some expectations you feel comfortable discussing and ensuring they understand, after which you can let go.

Start: Ready? Go back and re-review.

Were you able to identify some you can let go of? Can you have the conversation and then be done with an expectation topic?

As you know, there is no correct answer or magic expectation number. Your expectations will be about how you decide to balance your desired outcomes with their individual responsibility and growth. Ideally, they harness their maturity, street smarts and commitment and self-manage. Remember, the goal is for your child to become a successful, independent adult.

Pre-Departure Prep

No one knows your child better than you do. To that end, this next exercise, compiling a list of things you want to teach, advise, or discuss with your child before their departure, should be easy. We already know our expectations and can use our list as a point of reference for future discussion. Let's move on to the more tactical. One way to think about this is: what do you do for your child today which they cannot do for themselves? For example, when they were five years old, the answer would have been most everything (cooking, cleaning clothes, bathing, driving, managing money, shopping, teaching them everything). Now, they are about to launch into the world as adults. What do they need to learn to do on their own before they depart?

Exercise 2 – Basic Skills

Directions: Write down what you do for your child today that they don't know how to do themselves. You'll recall my number-one answer was managing money. Luckily, I found a way to teach them that with their departure. Since there are so many basic life skills, I can't possibly list them all. I'll start with a few, but you know better than I do what your child needs to know. For example, if they have a car, they need to know some basic things about car maintenance. But generically, here are a few basic survival skills necessary for life outside the home: laundry, cooking, cleaning, budgeting, banking, paying bills, managing time, and advocating for themselves.

Start: Create your list now.

Do you have a list? For a very independent child, this might be a concise list. For others, this may be a long list. The key is to think through basic skills and assess if they are ready to do this independently. One side note: your child may know how to wash sheets and make their bed, but do they know how often they need to change them? With some basic physical skills, there are also some common-sense parameters. Congratulations on having your pre-departure expectations and your child's basic skill readiness identified. Now, let's move on to discussion topics.

Exercise 3 – Discussion Topics

We each have diverse cultural backgrounds. Part of this diversity means that some children are potentially less aware, naive, or aren't as street-smart as others. This exercise aims to think through any topics you may want to discuss with your child before their departure. This could be personal safety and advice, sexual health and consent, alcohol and drugs, self-care, scams, academic integrity, or conflict management. Again, you know your child best. Take this moment to think about if your child may have some worldly blind spots or areas where they may not have a lot of experience. You can use my examples as a starting point.

Directions: Write down any discussion topics you feel your child may need to know or be refreshed on before they leave.

Start: Create your list.

Like the example of basic skills, I hope there isn't much. But if there are several topics your child would be more prepared with a deeper understanding, consider yourself more prepared now. You can take comfort in knowing that, by identifying some discussion topics to address, your departing child is about to become much more aware and self-sufficient. You'll recall there are three parts to your plan for your child:

346 THE EMPTY NEST BLUEPRINT FOR SINGLE PARENTS

pre-departure, communication, and your future parent-adult relationship. As we finish our pre-departure actions, let's focus on communication.

Communication

The entire premise of this book is that you become aware of your Empty Nest journey and take action. There are no aspects of this book where your child is asked, told, or expected to do anything. To that end, your work thus far is your plan for your child. It is not your child's plan that you hand to them, and they execute. That being said, the second part of your plan for your child does pull them into the conversation as a participant. First and foremost, the conversation about any of these items should be seen as a positive conversation you get to have where you share your excitement and support for their decision toward their destination. Whether it's off to college, the army, or a full-time job and an apartment, this is a time when you repeatedly get to build up their self-esteem. Let them know you are proud of them. Let them know you support them on their path forward. During this pre-departure period, you will want to discuss your expectations and what you want them to know, prepare for, and be equipped to handle. Most importantly, you want to underscore that they are loved and that you are excited for them.

It is tough for me to give you an example to sum up this topic or make up a conversation that would sound authentic.

The themes we have covered are your emotions, feelings, expectations, and discussion topics, which are more important than specific words. Your relationship with your child and the communication style you use with them will be whatever comes naturally. However, here is an example of what you may want to say in your own words or at least some themes you may want to cover:

- "I am so proud of you for pursuing your dreams and goals. I believe in you and know you will do great things."
- "Remember to always stay true to yourself and your values. Don't let anyone else influence your decisions or define your path in life."
- "Being away from home will be full of new experiences and challenges, but I know you are prepared to handle them. Don't be afraid to ask for help if you need it."
- "I will miss you, but I am excited about the journey you are about to embark on. Enjoy every moment and make the most of your time at college."
- "Remember that you are loved and always have a home to return to. I will be here to support you, no matter what."

Summed up, you love, trust, support, and acknowledge where they are in their journey and who they are.

It is essential to ensure you communicate what is important to you and them before and after they leave. Before they leave, if finances need to be discussed and shared, share

348 THE EMPTY NEST BLUEPRINT FOR SINGLE PARENTS

them. If you have expectations for them while they are away, explain them. If you have a pre-departure list you think they need to learn, share it with them. You have done the work; it is all about communicating what you discovered with them. If, upon completing the last few exercises, you have found you have a lot of topics to discuss with your child, my recommendation is that you break them up and discuss them over time. A one-time kitchen sink conversational topic dump will likely be overwhelming and not take hold.

The other communication consideration in your plan for your child concerns what you want to share with them. If you are comfortable, feel free to tell them how you are feeling, both the good and the bad, about your Empty Nest journey ahead. If there is worry, concern, or sadness, try to avoid putting guilt or pressure on them. Your happiness should never be their responsibility. If so inclined, you can share negative feelings with them, but do so confidently, noting that this is a period of adjustment for you both. Remember, you have also done considerable work understanding yourself and creating a future of excitement, fun, and joy. With this in mind, be open to sharing what you are looking forward to doing and how you plan to keep busy while they are gone. In the end, share with your child what you are comfortable sharing. Your plan for your child is an opportunity to ground yourself first, set expectations, gain advice and wisdom, and give them a lot of encouragement combined with your love and trust.

Parent-Adult Relationship

The final piece of your plan for your child is to think about what you want in your future parent-adult relationship. Chapter 8 explored the near-term parent-adult relationship as your child becomes more independent and responsible once they leave the home. Everything in this chapter underscores the beginning of this transition for you and your child. However, the future parent-adult relationship isn't created the day your child moves out but is developed over time. With this in mind, how you show up, support, love, and let go of your child will form your relationship with them as they move into adulthood. Like many other topics, there are better-equipped books on this subject that are rich with advice to explore.

I want to mention the longer-term parent-adult dynamic because how you interact with your departing child will set the tone for your parent-adult relationship in many ways. It sounds simple, but empowering them, supporting them, listening to them, and respecting them and their judgment will go a long way to keep them connected to you. You may find this time to be one of contrasts. Your adult child will not be your peer, but they sometimes want to be listened to and respected as if they are. Conversely, your adult child is no longer a child, yet they may need your nurturing and support as they once did. You are still and always will be their parent, just as they will be your child. Rather than suggesting you do specific things such as send them care packages of cookies, adopt the negotiables in chapter 8, or visit them twice a year, the best thing you can do for yourself is recognize that this is a time of their development and growth. Accepting this perspective will help you give them the distance, support, and love they need to advance their independence.

The longer-term goal of your plan for your child is to foster a healthy, loving parent-adult relationship, fostering deeper connection and stronger bonds long into the future. Congratulations! Your plan for your child is a great start in achieving this goal.

Other Plans

As a single parent, the most important plan is your own, followed by your child's. But I would be remiss if I didn't acknowledge that there are single-parent situations where others are deeply involved in your and your child's life. In these situations, having a plan for these individuals would be beneficial. I am not suggesting we create a detailed plan for everyone in your child's life. Still, a high-level game plan or seeing an Empty Nest transition from another perspective would be beneficial. Here are some other individuals and actions you can take to formulate an Empty Nest plan. I would only consider a plan for these additional people if they cohabitate with you and your child and have been actively involved in raising your child. Here is a list of potential other candidates for a plan:

- your ex
- your parents / your child's grandparents
- a part-time partner
- a close friend
- a roommate
- a close family member

Again, we are only considering creating a plan if any of these individuals lived with you and your child and have actively assisted you in raising your child. There is a term for this: alloparenting. An alloparent is an individual other than the biological parent of an offspring that performs the functions of a parent. To make things easier, I'll call this an alloparent plan. If this doesn't pertain to you, skip to the plan summary section.

Your Alloparent Plan

What would your plan for an alloparent look like? Your alloparent plan has two parts. The first part concerns your understanding, empathy, and awareness of what this person may be going through as your child departs. Just as your plan was about your emotional awareness and anticipation, this plan is about you identifying and being aware of your allowparent's emotions. Your understanding of the Empty Nest process will help you proactively identify and head off some of the negative feelings, pitfalls, or struggles that the alloparent may experience before anything happens. Again, this isn't a plan you assign to them. It is a plan that you have for yourself to support them in their journey. This part of the plan sits in your brain because it manifests as understanding, empathy, and awareness. You now get to apply everything you have learned and wanted for yourself to this other person. You essentially become their Empty Nest guide.

Here is how the first part of your plan for your alloparent becomes realized. It is a thought exercise. This is your opinion.

How do you believe they will experience their Empty Nest journey? You are welcome to write down answers or think through your thoughts.

___

Exercise 1 – Your Alloparent's Journey

Directions: Think through these statements and questions.

Start: Review the symptoms of Empty Nest Syndrome and ask yourself if you think the alloparent will potentially experience any symptoms. The symptoms are:

- **Loss of Identity**
- **Loss of Control**
- **Emotional Toll**
- **Relationship and Individual Stress**
- **Parenting Anxiety**

Each symptom can have multiple questions, such as:

- What concerns, if any, do you think the alloparent has about your child departing?
- How much of your alloparent's self-worth, time, active parenting, and life revolves around your child?
- Based on the alloparent's relationship with your child, how do you think their departure will affect them emotionally?

Think through the Empty Nest Threat examples and ask yourself where your alloparent is on each dimension. The threats are: depression, disownment, disconnection, and deprioritization

- Do you believe your alloparent will or has experienced any of these threats currently or once your child leaves? If so, which threat and why?
- Does your alloparent have a personal support structure?
- What does your alloparent need from you to support their journey?

This exercise aims to give you an emotional profile of what you believe your alloparent may feel and encounter with their Empty Nest journey. Your plan for your alloparent is anticipating how they may react to all the aspects of their Empty Nest journey (your child's departure) and how you can use your insight to support them. It makes no difference if your assumptions were 100 percent correct or wrong. Your plan for your alloparent is built on your desire to empathize with and support them. Once you complete the second part of your plan for them, introducing the Empty Nest journey and your thoughts with them, your pre-work will pay off.

Getting Your Alloparent on Board

The second part of your plan centers around interaction with your alloparent to help them with their journey. The simple goal is to get alloparents to think actively through their Empty Nest transition. The easiest way to do this is to hand them this book and make them read it. Trust me, I understand that reading a book someone hands you often conflicts with one's time, priorities, and interests. If they don't drop everything and dive into this book, you must execute your plan for them the old-fashioned way with one-on-one communication.

You can approach the Empty Nest subject with an alloparent in a million ways. There are many, but I don't want to get bogged down with examples. I do, however, have two suggestions.

My first suggestion is to have the conversation at a time and a place where you think they can process and think. It may not be the best time to begin this discussion at a sporting event or when they are exhausted. Find a window when you fully have their attention, and the possibility of interruption is minimized.

My second suggestion is to consider how your alloparent processes information. Do you want to introduce the subject, give them time to think about it, and then have a conversation? Or do you feel they will be comfortable having the conversation on the spot? You know the person who has been helping you raise your child better than anyone else, so pick a time and approach when and where you feel the conversation will best be served.

Your plan for your alloparent is to help them think about the emotions and feelings they will have around the upcoming departure of your child. You might be inclined to introduce questions such as:

- "What do you think your life will be like once Jimmy leaves the home?"
- "What are you looking forward to? Do you have any concerns? If so, what are they?"
- "Do you have any anxiety, sadness, or dread?"

Remember, they likely have not thought through any of these topics, and they may not be prepared to articulate them on the spot. Instead of sitting down and drilling them with many questions, a better way to broach this subject is to share your thoughts. Share your big takeaways on the topic of becoming an empty nester. Share your thoughts and concerns. Share your expectations. Share components of your plan. Most importantly, share your excitement with all the positives you put in your plan. It's as easy as, "I have been thinking a lot lately about Johnny's departure. I have been feeling… (this way).

I think this is an opportunity for us to… (insert positives) because we will have more time. I am excited about…"

As you share your feelings and thoughts, pause for a moment and ask them what they think. Do they have any of the same thoughts and emotions? If you think it would be better to ease into their thought process and not jump into emotions, ask them less vulnerable questions, such as:

- "If you had more free time on nights and weekends, what would you want to do?"
- "Do you believe Johnny is ready to be on his own?"
- "Do you have any worries or concerns about Johnny leaving or living on his own?"
- "Are you excited about your life once Johnny leaves?"

Your plan for your alloparent isn't necessarily about their answers. Remember, your plan is not to have them tell you what you want to hear, adapt your thinking, or develop their plan. They will inevitably not be in the same place or mindset you are in since you have had the benefit of reading this book and reflecting throughout each chapter. Shoot, you have even made your plans. You are much further ahead than anyone when it comes to understanding and thinking through an Empty Nest journey. With this insight, temper your expectations.

Again, their answers during this introduction to the Empty Nest topic aren't critical. What is important is that you have successfully introduced the subject to them. In doing so, you have triggered them to think about their emotions and their place at this stage of their life. Once you have done this, you can bring the subject back up, check in, and discuss it with them at any time.

Your plan for your alloparent is to think through the Empty Nest journey from their perspective based on everything you know about them. Explore all the intricacies you believe they will encounter and experience as an alloparent. Then introduce the Empty Nest subject to them to get them thinking about their future. Help them understand all the aspects of the transition. If you do these two things, your plan for your alloparent will have been fulfilled.

Plan Summary

I almost started this chapter with the definition of a plan. Instead, I decided to include the definition in the closing to underscore what you have done. According to Webster's Dictionary, a plan is "a detailed proposal for doing or achieving something." As you started this chapter and even this book, your Empty Nest goal was to, "Navigate Your New Normal and Thrive for the Most Underrated Stage of Your Life."

I hope you agree that, without a plan to focus on your Empty Nest journey, the entire transition would be left up to chance. Like so many other single parents before you, your child's departure, emotions and perspective, and future journey would have continued naturally through daily routine. Your experience would be to "shoot from the hip" and hope things turn out well. Without a plan, the possibilities of thriving are left up to chance. This is no longer the case for you. With your plans, the advantages and assurances of thriving as an empty nester are greater.

I want to congratulate you on getting to this point. You have done much work and prioritized yourself and your child for a better future. Whether your plans are all in your head, scribbled in the margins, or neatly typed in a three-ring binder, you have invested your time and effort in setting up your relationships and your Empty Nest journey toward the best possible outcome.

CHAPTER 16 KEY POINTS

- Your plan for your child is the second most important plan after your own.

- Each plan you create is your plan. They are not plans for your child to execute but rather what you will do for them.

- The cornerstone of each plan is empathizing, supporting, and helping yourself or someone else through their next stage of life.

- Your Empty Nest Opportunities, exercises, and plans culminate in you creating a Blueprint for your best Empty Nest life.

"A single parent has a backbone made of steel and a heart made of gold."

—ANONYMOUS

CONCLUSION

IN MY FIRST forty-five years on this planet, I never considered, worried about, or had a fleeting thought about my Empty Nest life. There was the evolution of having a family, an ongoing career, and retirement far out in the distance. I was doing what we all do, going about my daily routine, letting life's experiences wash over me in the moment. My default, perhaps for survival or sanity's sake, was to live with routine.

However, when we think about achieving important things, we know they require more effort, such as accomplishing a lifelong goal or making an important decision.

In these instances, we tend to break away from the routine, evaluate our options, and plan more carefully. For life's biggest moments, many of which are relationship-based milestones, the savvy among us invest whatever time is necessary to ensure that our choices and efforts have the most beneficial outcome.

This is precisely what you have done for yourself by reading this book. As I did, you have recognized that your journey as an empty nester is essential. It is a major relationship-based transition in life, allowing you to reset and build the future you want. You have prioritized yourself and your child by focusing on your Empty Nest life. I applaud your efforts in reading this book and working through the exercises. You have accomplished a lot. Let me take one more moment of your time and lay it all out for you.

First, you have gained an understanding of the research, pitfalls, and challenges single empty nesters face. With this insight alone, I believe you can help yourself, your friends, and your family members by being aware, empathetic, and understanding of the threats and opportunities of their Empty Nest journeys. This alone is a pretty amazing insight that you now possess.

Beyond expanding your knowledge and understanding of the subject, you have done much more for yourself. You have evaluated your past, your parenting influences, and your relationships. This reflection and understanding has empowered you to see yourself and your relationships in a new light.

You have thought through your and your child's transition from parent-child to parent-adult. You have insights into their journey and actions you can take to help them prepare and thrive as they leave the nest. Through this discovery, your decisions, actions, and approach toward your child in the future will be more informed and lead to better outcomes. The self-discovery gift you just gave yourself will be a lifelong gift for you and your child.

By exploring symptoms and solutions and understanding the threats and the opportunities, your introspection while reading this book has brought forth an Empty Nest relevancy. Your insights into your Empty Nest journey laid the foundation for you to create a personalized blueprint. By completing the exercises and focusing your efforts, you now possess a minimum of two plans that will help you do the following:

- Have a positive Empty Nest perspective and journey.
- Help your child transition after leaving the home.
- Help your parent-child relationship successfully transition into parent-adult.
- Help to ensure your future is fun, exciting, and filled with joy.

Again, you have accomplished a lot. Congratulations!

My Empty Nest journey has been successful due to a change in my mindset and planning. My resolve to create the Empty Nest future I wanted has enabled me to do just that. My life, like everyone else's, is not perfect. I am not the ideal spouse with the perfect marriage or a perfect father with perfect children. There is a reason this book isn't titled *Empty Nest Perfection for the Single Parent,* because that is unreachable. Author David Perlmutter said, "Strive for progress, not perfection." I approach each day of my Empty Nest life with this mindset.

I work toward making my parent-adult relationships with my children meaningful and rich by seeing opportunity in every interaction. I focus on living a fun-filled and exciting future by planning, introducing, and taking any actions to support living my best life. I also realize that, unless I prioritize my health and happiness in parallel with the other critical relationships in my life, I won't be able to be there for others.

I am grateful for my Empty Nest journey, my relationships, and my outlook on the future every day. I wholeheartedly believe that you can have a successful Empty Nest journey. You have the resolve, the knowledge, and the plans to thrive as an individual and in your relationships as you move beyond your child-rearing years.

May your Empty Nest journey be all it can be— filled with excitement, fun, and joy!

AFTERWORD

I STARTED THIS book by researching everything I could find on being a single parent in the United States. Although there is a lot of data, surveys, and articles on being a single parent with children under eighteen, I found almost no data on being a single parent after your child or children turn eighteen. There is a lot of data on single adults, but this category includes anyone who isn't married, regardless of their status as a parent. As I researched single parenting, my respect and admiration for this parent class grew. Achieving goals that pertain to finances, home ownership, career advancement, and health is statistically easier and more attainable when two people are involved. Raising a child solo requires immense sacrifice and strength. When you step back and think of the enormity of decisions, responsibilities, and actions needed to raise a child today, single parents' dedication pushes the boundaries of what we can all achieve. I sincerely believe that single parents are a testament to human potential, and it is my hope that this book will support that belief.

As your Empty Nest future takes shape, I encourage you to connect with me at AnthonyDamaschino.com. On this website, you will find additional resources and content to help support you on your Empty Nest journey. Feel free to subscribe to my newsletter, take an Empty Nest readiness test, or join in on the single empty nester statistics by taking a survey. If you enjoyed this book, I would appreciate you taking a few moments to write a review on the platform where you purchased the book. Please leave an Amazon review if the book was a gift or a library check-out. Doing this is the kindest thing you can do beyond purchasing a book for any author. I am grateful for your support. Thank you!

I sincerely hope that your investment in this book, and more importantly, yourself and your relationships, has catalyzed a more rewarding future.

Let's live our best Empty Nest lives.

ACKNOWLEDGMENTS

THIS BOOK WOULDN'T have been possible without the help of all the single parents I spoke with and the many anonymous single empty nester survey participants. I cannot thank you all personally, but your contribution toward understanding this subject and this book will surely help others. For that, you have my sincere gratitude. I thank my editor, Nate Best, for transforming my words into a compelling book. I also want to thank George at G Sharp Design for being a great cover and book designer and an advocate and friend.

To my wife Karen and my three children, Everest, Grace, and Zoe, although this book is close to seventy thousand words, no words can express my love for each of you. Thank you to Rea Roberts and Amy Zeifang for being the first and current fan club presidents. Mom, thanks again for always being there for me and championing me throughout my life.

As I said in the Acknowledgments for my last book, I am endlessly grateful for my family and friends. Clarence was right: "Remember, no man is a failure who has friends." To all my friends and family, thank you for putting up with me. Life is so much richer when you can experience it with deep and valued relationships.

NOTES

Badiani, Feryl & Desousa, Avinash. (2016). The Empty Nest Syndrome: Critical Clinical Considerations. Indian Journal of Mental Health (IJMH), 3, 135. DOI: 10.30877/ IJMH.3.2.2016.135-142

Baumrind, D. (1991). Parenting styles and adolescent development. In J. Brooks-Gunn, R. M. Lerner, & A. C. Petersen (Eds.), The encyclopedia on adolescence (pp. 746-758). New York: Garland Publishing.

Bougea, A., Despoti, A., & Vasilopoulos, E. (2020). Empty-nest-related psychosocial stress: Conceptual issues, future directions in economic crisis. Psychiatrikī, 30(4), 329–338. DOI: 10.22365/ jpsych.2019.304.329

Bureau of Labor Statistics. American Time Use Survey [Internet]. Available from: https://www.bls.gov/news.release/pdf/atus.pdf

Bureau of Labor Statistics. Family Time and Expenditures: 2022 [Internet]. Available from: https://www.bls.gov/news.release/pdf/famee.pdf

Centers for Disease Control and Prevention. Teen Pregnancy [Internet]. Available from: https://www.cdc.gov/teenpregnancy/about/index.htm

Census Bureau. (2022, November 17). For Immediate Release: Thursday, November 17, 2022 Census Bureau Releases New Estimates on America's Families and Living Arrangements. Retrieved from https://www.census.gov/newsroom/press-releases/2022/americas-families-and-living-arrangements.html

Cohen, L. J. (2019, September 27). The authoritative parenting style: An evidence-based guide. Parenting Science. Retrieved from: https:// www.parentingscience.com/authoritative-parenting-style.html

Damaschino, A. (2024, January 2). Single Parent Empty Nest Survey. Retrieved from https://docs.google.com/forms/d/e/1FAIpQLSdA_7JkY1zXHFjAzAOKktvYOTL15pJqJHIObaQ8KpcLu-jk6Aviewform?vc=0&c=0&w=1&flr=0

Esri. (2021). LifeMode Group: GenXurban Comfortable empty nesters. Retail:360. Retrieved from https://retail360.us/dashboard/psychographics/5A_ComfortableEmptyNesters.pdf

Families in the United States. (2023, May 31). Statista. https://www.statista.com/topics/1484/families/#dossierKeyfigures

Fidelity Investments. (2022). Fidelity Investments® 2022 College Savings Indicator. Retrieved from https://www.fidelity.com/bin-public/060_ www_fidelity_com/documents/about-fidelity/FidelityInvestments2022CollegeSavingsIndicator.pdf

Fitelson, E., Kim, S. E., Baker, A. H., & Leight, K. (2010). Treatment of post-partum depression: a review of clinical, psychological and pharmacological options. International Journal of Women's Health, 1, 1-14. Retrieved from https://doi.org/10.2147/ijwh.s6938

GoodTherapy. How to Cope with Empty Nest Syndrome When You're a Single Parent [Internet]. 2019 May 31. Available from: https://www.goodtherapy.org/blog/how-to-cope-with-empty-nest-syndrome-when-youre-a-single-parent-0531198

Health eUniversity. (n.d.). Sense of Control. Retrieved from https://www.healtheuniversity.ca/EN/CardiacCollege/Wellbeing/Stress_And_Sense_Of_Control/Pages/sense-of-control.aspx

HealthyChildren.org. (n.d.). Everybody Gets Mad: Helping Your Child Cope with Conflict. Retrieved from https://www.healthychildren.org/English/healthy-living/emotional-wellness/Pages/Everybody-Gets-Mad-Helping-Your-Child-Cope-with-Conflict.aspx

Higuera, V. (2023, March 24). Everything You Need to Know About Depression (Major Depressive Disorder). Healthline. https://www.healthline.com/health/depression

Markham, L. (2014, September 9). Authoritative Versus Authoritarian Parenting Style. Aha! Parenting. Retrieved from https://www.ahaparenting.com/parenting-tools/positive-discipline/Authoritative-Parenting-Style

Merrill Lynch. The Financial Journey of Modern Parenting [Internet]. 2023 Mar 8. Available from: https://www.ml.com/the-financial-journey-of-modern-parenting.html

MedicalXpress. (2017, October). How you can enjoy the 'best of the best' of the world's healthiest foods. Retrieved from https://medicalxpress.com/news/2017-10-how-you-can-enjoy-the.html

Mintel. (2021). US Marketing to empty nesters Market Report. Retrieved from https://store.mintel.com/report/us-marketing-to-empty-nesters-market-report

Monte, L. M. (2017). Counting the Chicks after They've Flown: Shared and Non-Shared Fertility Among empty nesters. Presented at the Annual Meeting of the Population Association of America, Chicago, IL, April 27-29, 2017.

Optimist. (2022, August 2). 71% of empty nesters Will Renovate Their Homes—Neighbor Blog. Neighbor Blog. https://www.neighbor.com/storage-blog/empty-nesters-renovate-homes/

Population Reference Bureau. Do Parents Spend Enough Time with Their Children? [Internet]. Available from: https://www.prb.org/resources/do-parents-spend-enough-time-with-their-children/ Psych Central. (n.d.). Empty Nest Syndrome. Retrieved from https://psychcentral.com/health/empty-nest-syndrome

Raup, J. L., & Myers, J. E. (1989). The Empty Nest Syndrome: Myth or Reality? Journal of Counseling and Development, 68(2), 180–183. DOI: 10.1002/j.1556-6676.1989.tb01353.x

Robinson, K. M. (2021, July 12). What Is Situational Depression? WebMD. https://www.webmd.com/depression/situational-depression

Saving for college in the U.S. (2022, April 8). Statista. https://www.statista.com/topics/1561/saving-for-college-in-the-us/#topicOverview

Seitzer, M. (2019). Adult Children: The Guide to Parenting Your Grown Kids. New Harbinger Publications. (Updated 2022).

Stanford Children's Health. Give 'Em Some Skin: The Importance of Physical Touch for Your Child's Development [Internet]. Available from: https://www.stanfordchildrens.org/en/health-topics/magazine/give-em-some-skin

Statista. Number of children living with a single mother or single father in the United States from 1960 to 2023 [Internet]. Available from: https://www.statista.com/statistics/252847/number-of-children-living-with-a-single-mother-or-single-father/

Statista Research Department. (2023, January 20). Share of family households with own children under 18 years in the United States from 1970 to 2021, by type of family. Statista. Retrieved from https://www.statista.com/statistics/242074/percentages-of-us-family-households-with-children-by-type/

Terrazas, A. (2017, April 19). Empty Nest Households Are on the Rise. Zillow Research. Retrieved from https://www.zillow.com/research/empty-nests-rise-14810/

United States of America Demographics—Place Explorer—Data Commons. (n.d.). Retrieved from: https://datacommons.org/place/c

Wang, C.; Zhang, B.; Oláh, J.; Hasan, M. Factors Influencing the Quality of Life of empty nesters: Empirical Evidence from Southwest China. Sustainability 2021, 13, 2662. https://doi.org/10.3390/su13052662

World Animal Foundation. (2024). How Long Do Birds Stay in the Nest? Retrieved from https://www.birdsandblooms.com/birding/attracting-birds/bird-nesting/how-long-baby-birds-stay-nest/

55places.com Survey. (2019, March 11). Survey Reveals empty nesters Still Supporting Children Financially. Retrieved from https://www.55places.com/blog/survey-reveals-empty-nesters-still-supporting-children-financially

ABOUT THE AUTHOR

ANTHONY DAMASCHINO, a devoted father of three and self-proclaimed recovering HR executive turned author, brings a wealth of personal, professional, and data-based experience to his writing. When he's not at his local library writing about parenting, midlife relationships, or personal development, he can be found out in nature, impersonating an accomplished hiker. Anthony lives in Northern California, where he too is on the journey to embrace life's endless experiences and possibilities.

www.ingramcontent.com/pod-product-compliance
Lightning Source LLC
Chambersburg PA
CBHW060854120626
46553CB00001B/79